The Gurdjieff Work

by

Kathleen Riordan Speeth

Illustrated by Thommy Davis

AND/OR PRESS
BERKELEY, CALIFORNIA
1976

Published and distributed by AND/OR PRESS
P.O. Box 2246
Berkeley, CA 94702

ISBN No. 0-915904-19-5

Printed in USA
First Printing September 1976

Second Printing April 1977

Quotes from *In Search of the Miraculous*
by P.D. Ouspensky, copyright, 1949, by Harcourt
Brace Jovanovich, Inc. and reprinted
with their permission.

The Sacred traditions of the world define the aims and values of a good life, inspire moral sentiments and the highest ideals of which mankind is capable. Each of the great religions has an esoteric aspect in which methods for learning to actually live by these values are transmitted orally to specially prepared aspirants. G.I. Gurdjieff, a contemporary of Sigmund Freud, gained access to the hidden wisdom of Eastern and Western sacred technologies and formulated a body of teachings for use by present-day European and American seekers of self-realization. His system has rarely been taught outside closed groups of already committed students. Here at last is a clearly presented, concise introduction to his life, his work, and his ideas.

G. I. Gurdjieff: Philosopher, Explorer, and Master of Dancing.

To the Beloved
many-formed,
who, whenever I notice, is always guiding me.

TOTILLA ALBERT ☆☆☆ AMMA ☆☆☆ FRANK BARRON ☆☆☆ MARINA BEAR ☆☆☆ LUC BREBION ☆☆☆ JOE CAMHI ☆☆☆ CARLOS CASTANEDA ☆☆☆ AKAI COULTER ☆☆☆ SULEYMAN DEDE ☆☆☆ OLGA DE HARTMANN ☆☆☆ ROBERT DE ROPP ☆☆☆ JEANNE DE SALZMANN ☆☆☆ DHIRAVAMSA ☆☆☆ BOBBY DREYFUS ☆☆☆ ALFRED ETIERVANT ☆☆☆ LISE ETIER-VANT ☆☆☆ JIM FADIMAN ☆☆☆ RESHAD FEILD ☆☆☆ BOB FRAGER ☆☆☆ IRA FRIEDLANDER ☆☆☆ DATTARAM GAVAND ☆☆☆ E.J. GOLD ☆☆☆ GEORGE GURDJIEFF ☆☆☆ JIM HARRIS ☆☆☆ CLIFFORD HERSH ☆☆☆ BOB HOFFMAN ☆☆☆ JESSMIN HOWARTH ☆☆☆ ESTELLE HOYT ☆☆☆ DON HOYT ☆☆☆ OSCAR ICHAZO ☆☆☆ H.H. KARMAPA ☆☆☆ AL KASTL ☆☆☆ SAM KEEN ☆☆☆ FRED KELLER ☆☆☆ FIONA KLINE ☆☆☆ HENRY KORMAN ☆☆☆ JACK KORNFIELD ☆☆☆ MARK KRIGER ☆☆☆ J. KRISH-NAMURTI ☆☆☆ MICHAEL LORIMER ☆☆☆ GAY LUCE ☆☆☆ LEON LURIE ☆☆☆ STUART MARGULIES ☆☆☆ ALAN MARX ☆☆☆ ARMANDO MOLINA ☆☆☆ LARRY MORRIS ☆☆☆ BABA MUKTANANDA ☆☆☆ DULCIE MURPHY ☆☆☆ CHARLES MUSES ☆☆☆ CLAUDIO NARANJO ☆☆☆ JAVAD NURBAKHSH ☆☆☆ WILLEM NYLAND ☆☆☆ DEBORA O'KEEFE ☆☆☆ LAURA PERLS ☆☆☆ BEATRICE RAFF ☆☆☆ PAUL REYNARD ☆☆☆ DUDJOM RINPOCHE ☆☆☆ GYATRUL RINPOCHE ☆☆☆ TAR-THANG RINPOCHE ☆☆☆ JOHN RIORDAN ☆☆☆ MAVIS MCIN-TOSH RIORDAN ☆☆☆ DAVID ROSENMANN ☆☆☆ HASSAN SHUSHUD ☆☆☆ HAKIM SKELLY ☆☆☆ SHELDON SKLARE ☆☆☆ LAUREN SPEETH ☆☆☆ CATHERINE SWINARSKI ☆☆☆ TAJ ☆☆☆ PAMELA TRAVERS ☆☆☆ VIRGINIA VEACH ☆☆☆ WILLIAM WELCH ☆☆☆ LOUISE WELCH ☆☆☆ BOB HORN ☆☆☆

Foreword

Gurdjieff's place in the world of spiritual teachings and teachers is mysterious, intriguing and definitely very important. Truly he was—to borrow his expression from a booklet written during his sojourn in France—a herald of the coming good. Today when what was once esoteric is coming into the marketplace and into practically everybody's life, and when the *barakath* is affecting the thousands, it may take some effort of imagination to empathize with the predicament of this man, an initiate of an ancient esoteric school who took it upon himself to show the Western world that mankind is asleep, that there are higher levels of being, and that there are somewhere people who know. He certainly had the background and the gift to extract the essence of many teachings and to present it clean of cultural trappings or accretions in a way appropriate to the situation he was in. One of the enigmas about him is the contrast between his seeming mastery and his failure to elevate, in the course of his lifetime, any of his disciples to his level —and thus to found a tradition in the full measure of the term. Yet he did not fail, as we judge him not by his teaching of the few but from his role in the history of culture and spirituality. As a single individual he managed to administer the European and American world a shock perhaps more significant than any other until the cultural wave of the early sixties.

Kathleen Riordan Speeth was born into the Gurdjieff work, in which her parents had already been immersed for 13 years; experienced the master's unalterable sweetness toward children (and abrasiveness with grownups) and has been absorbing his ideas in theory and practice ever since. Her exploration of other teaching situations in recent years, furthermore, gives her a perspective that is rare in the Gurdjieff literature, and she has now presented what is a clear and concise account of the master's chief ideas. May it stimulate the reader's conscious labors and purifying sufferings.

—Claudio Naranjo
Albany, California, July, 1976

Preface

An atmosphere of clandestine meetings in revolutionary circumstances still pervades the activities of many of the followers of
Gurdjieff. At a time when the most esoteric tantric teachings are
available in paperback, when Sufi stories are selling to the millions,
when politicians find it permissible and even valuable to visit Indian
gurus, certain public figures, authors and lecturers connected with
Gurdjieff's ideas, will never, never state their connections with the
work publicly. Nor will I unmask them. That is for each one of us
to do according to our own understanding.

All I can do is to unmask myself as best I know how, for it is
my belief that readers have a right to know where an author is coming from. Books are written by human beings and human beings inevitably have biases.

Gurdjieff has been an influence in my life from before the beginning, and I have yet to untangle all the threads of intellectual
and emotional identification that still bind me to him. I was born
into the Gurdjieff work and bear its mark. Somewhere Gurdjieff
is quoted as saying that each person's religion must be honored for
hidden within its dogma is his or her conscience: deeply, I know
that whatever in me registers truth, goodness and beauty is surrounded with associations of Gurdjieff's teachings and his person.
His warm cheek, his barely comprehensible, Rabelaisian remarks,
his incredible generosity, his poignant music—what I know of love
carries this imprint.

The basic pattern of threefoldness, the trinity, appears most
intimately to us in the family—in mother, father and child. In our
times the child loves its parents unrequitedly. Their backs are
turned for they are still looking toward their own parents for the
love they never received. (Sometimes I envision the whole of kali
yuga humanity marching backward into the future, lined up this
way.) And I am sure that my affection for and attachment to my
own mother and father, both students of Orage and Gurdjieff,

have contributed to my almost obsessive preoccupation with the
Gurdjieff literature, my spiritual materialism in the pursuit of witness
consciousness, and my search for a teacher of Gurdjieff's stature.

When Charles Tart asked me to contribute a chapter on Gurdjieff for his book, *Transpersonal Psychologies,* several years ago, it
seemed an appropriate moment to review what I knew of the work
for my own purposes. I was then immersed in a study of my life as
part of a group activity directed by Claudio Naranjo. We were using
a very powerful system of ego typology transmitted by Oscar Ichazo, a system that threw the outlines of my chief feature into unde-
niable high relief. Part of the suffering that seems inevitable in
such work was due in my case to the realization that my habitual
functioning was organized around a central flaw or distortion of
the truth that had much to do with a wrong understanding of Gurdjieff's ideas. The devil, a subtle theologian, was whispering to me in
the language of the work! I had to understand where the truth was
and where it was not. The research that went into the chapter in
Tart's book served me well in that regard.

The present volume grew out of that chapter in response to
several requests to use the article in college classes. As part of the
large collection of articles in *Transpersonal Psychologies* it could
not easily be made available to those who wanted, not a survey,
but an introduction to Gurdjieff's teachings. I saw the need for a
Gurdjieff primer, so to speak. Preparing such a book seemed like an
opportunity to give the human potential movement something
simple, relevant and free of the patriarchal language and anecdotal
ramblings that colored earlier works. It would also, I reasoned,
give me more contact with the Gurdjieff heritage that I must somehow fully metabolize.

Perhaps this new rendition is still too academic. Most of the
writing I have done has been in anonymous communal efforts for
college audiences and my style may still suffer from the rigidity of
that genre. I have wished to give the reader a sense of the heart and
the life of the work rather than a recital of the Gurdjieff catechism.
I think I may have partially fulfilled my aim in putting more than
a decade of earnest Gurdjieff groups and effortful Gurdjieff week-
ends behind me and offering my own understanding. If I have suc-
ceeded in transmitting something living it must be due to my parents' early attempts to leave me free; to the real contact I sometimes had with the many teachers within the Gurdjieff Foundation
whose names I omit out of respect for their desire to remain hidden;

to Claudio Naranjo who has for five years inspired, enriched and mercilessly scourged me; to David Rosenmann who embodies the pattern my heart is yearning for; to Baba Muktananda who breathed life into me in his limitless compassion; to His Holiness Gyalwa Karmapa who gave me his blessing; to Tarthang Tulku, Rinpoche who is a natural mirror; to my present fourth way teacher who revolutionized my situation and to my students and patients who teach me about human nature and somehow make me their channel.

I am delighted by the drawings of my friend, Thommy Davis, which were created while listening to a recording of Gurdjieff improvising on the harmonium. I would like to acknowledge the collaboration of Day Chapin, who labored over the rest of the graphics, and Ricia Wise who typed the manuscript. The production of the book is one of the good works of Carlene Schnabel, without whose efforts this octave could not have come to completion.

–Kathleen Riordan Speeth
Albany, California
August, 1976

Contents

Chapter 1: Who Was Gurdjieff?   3

"The Work" / Gurdjieff's Quest / Early Preparation / Religious & Eso-
teric Fertility of His Native Land / The Search for Sources of Eternal
Wisdom / His Various Occupations, Business Enterprises and Political
Involvement / The Russian Period / Gurdjieff in Europe / The Later Years

Chapter 2: The Philosophical Basis of Gurdjieff's System   19

Self-Realization and the Human Condition / The Ray of Creation / The
Law of Three and The Law of Seven / The Law of Octave / The Ennea-
gram: The Union of the Law of Seven and the Law of Three / The First
Conscious Shock / The Second Conscious Shock

Chapter 3: The Psychology of Ordinary Human Beings   31

Human Fragmentation / The Human Machine / Our "Three Brains" /
Three Human Types / States of Consciousness / The Psychopathology
of Ordinary Waking State / The Systematic Distortion of Experience of
Ordinary Waking State / Essence and Personality

Chapter 4: Human Possibilities   51

Potential for Inner Growth / The Four Ways / Higher States of Consciousness / Objective Consciousness / Peak Experiences / The Stages of Human Development / Achieving Inner Unity / The Seven Levels / Evolution, Death and Immortality / Development of the Four Bodies

Chapter 5: The Gurdjieff Work   69

Engaging the Struggle Between Essence and Personality / The Beginning /
Stages on the Way / Finding a Group / The First Line of Work / Self-
Remembering / The Second Line of Work / External Considering / Non-
Expression of Negative Emotions / The Third Line of Work / Selfless
Action / The Movements / Breaking the Cycle of Lifelong Conditioning /
The Role of Physical Labor in the Work / Experiential Exercises

Chapter 6: The Living Tradition   95

The Gurdjieff Foundations / Sherborne and Claymont / Taliesen / The
Church of the Earth / East Hill Farm / A.I.C.E. / The Institute for Religious Development / Mme. de Hartmann's Group / Other Groups

Further Reading   107

Notes   109

The Gurdjieff Work

Man is asleep, must he die before he wakes?

—Saying of Mohammed

If a man could understand all the horror of the lives of ordinary people who are turning round in a circle of insignificant interests and insignificant aims, if he could understand what they are losing, he would understand that there can only be one thing that is serious for him—to escape from the general law, to be free. What can be serious for a man in prison who is condemned to death? Only one thing: How to save himself, how to escape: nothing else is serious.

—G.I. Gurdjieff

CHAPTER ONE:
Who Was Gurdjieff?

In most parts of the Western world you can, if you make a serious attempt to do so, find a group of people who are, as they say, "in the work"—that is, who attempt, together and as individuals, to function more consciously and harmoniously according to the ideas and practices given by George Ivanovich Gurdjieff. Gurdjieff groups generally avoid publicity. They do not proselytize. They are relatively invisible in the world, being as hard to find as a particular piece of hay in a haystack because their members lead ordinary lives while devoting themselves to their inner work. This work was developed to take a human being the whole way to his or her fullest potential—that is, all the way to liberation. It is designed to engage many aspects of human functioning and involves a wide range of activities including intellectual study, self observation, daily meditation, sacred dances or "movements," cooperative efforts and, more often than not, arts, crafts or manual labor, undertaken in special conditions.

The extraordinary being and "rascal sage" to whom all this activity is due devoted his life to understanding the great religious traditions, culling from each the secret oral teachings and translating them into forms that could be assimilated by contemporary Western seekers. Gurdjieff was quite successful in creating a fog around himself during his lifetime, just as don Juan, another man of knowledge, was to recommend to all who tread the path.[1] No one who encountered him face to face during his teaching years doubted that he was an extraordinary being—but who was he? An avatar, whose teachings were self-contained and self-validating? Or a teacher who was in contact with the source of his teaching, as he once warned a disciple that all authentic teachers must be? Like the Buddhists, he taught man to see his karma, his suffering, his own nothingness, and he demonstrated the inextricable interrelationship of all things. Like the Hindus, he gave the hope of devel·

oping higher levels of being and moving closer to the endlessness beyond all separation through austere techniques of mind and body control. Like the Sufis, he was in the world, but not of it, transmitting his extraordinary teaching situationally, often over seemingly ordinary activities, as the time, the place and the people required. Yet, although his teaching reflected influences from many of the world's sacred traditions, he was born and died a Russian Orthodox Christian. How did Gurdjieff come to the understanding that changed his own life and that of so many others? Although he did not make things easy for his future biographers, some information can be pieced together from more or less reliable sources and from these bits and pieces, the pattern of his life emerges.

GURDJIEFF'S QUEST

Gurdjieff was born in the 1870s in Alexandropol, in the Caucasus region of what is now Russia, of a Greek father and an Armenian mother. Although his passport date of birth was November 28th, 1877, his own reports of his age and the events of his life point to an earlier birthdate, probably around 1872. While he was still a boy his family moved to the nearby town of Kars, where he had the good fortune to study with the dean of the Russian military cathedral who, with Gurdjieff's own father, became an important influence on his development. According to Gurdjieff, these two men were chiefly responsible for the early arousal of an " '. . . irrepressible striving' to understand clearly the precise significance, in general, of the life process on earth of all outward forms of breathing creatures and, in particular, of the aim of human life in the light of this interpretation."[2] What are we living for? What is at the end of it all, at death? Gurdjieff was impressed as a youth with certain inexplicable events for which his elders could offer only uncertain opinions. He was present at a table-tapping seance after his young sister's death; watched a paralytic walk again at a saint's tomb; experienced uncanny accuracy in the predictions of a fortune teller; witnessed a miraculous cure that resulted from medical advice received in a dream; heard of a Tartar corpse that walked after death. He himself had tried to drag a Yezidi out of a magic circle from which he could not escape, only to find that once out, the victim fell into a cataleptic trance. He experimented with hypnosis until he mastered the art. The lack of complete and exact understanding of such phenomena by his respected teachers and tutors led Gurdjieff to a deep inner wish to develop a clear and comprehensive understanding of all aspects of human existence.

To this end he prepared for a vocation as a physician and

priest, studying in particular every available work on neurophysiol-
ogy and psychology: the libraries did not contain what he was looking for. Convinced that there had been at some time, somewhere,
schools or communities with real knowledge and that if so, this
inner circle of humanity might still exist, he made contact with
many diverse secret societies and religious groups, gaining access
to "the so-called holy-of-holies of nearly all hermetic organizations
such as religious, philosophical, occult, political and mystic societies, congregations, parties, unions, etc. which were inaccessible
to the ordinary man, and of discussing and exchanging views with
innumerable people who, in comparison with others, are real
authorities."[3] He lived in an area that was particularly rich ground
for unearthing answers to perennial questions, or at least for dig-
ging up clues. Kars and the surrounding region lying between the
Black and Caspian Seas is a natural migratory route where Europe
and Asia intermingle. It had been invaded and occupied by many
different peoples and was, during Gurdjieff's formative years, a
place of great cultural ferment owing to the interpenetration of
traditions of Christian, Armenian, Assyrian, Islamic and even Zoro-
astrian origins.

Gurdjieff gathered much in his native land, particularly from
Christian monastic sources. Very much later in his life, when he
had begun to teach; he was asked about the relation of Christianity
to the system of self-development he was offering to his students.

> "I do not know what you know about *Christianity*," answered
> G., emphasizing the word. "It would be necessary to talk a great
> deal and to talk for a long time in order to make clear what you
> understand by the term. But for the benefit of those who know al-
> ready, I will say that, if you like, *this is esoteric Christianity*."[4]

There was considerable knowledge about Christian ritual and practice to be had in Kars and Gurdjieff apparently learned much about
the ancient symbolism of the liturgy and the techniques of rhythmic breathing and mental prayer that were still part of the orthodox monk's religious duty. Yet, despite the fertility of his native
land and the religious tradition into which he had been born, he
was not at all satisfied with the progress of his understanding of the
basic question he had posed himself. He went in search of knowledge.

In the course of his attempts to find the remnants, the descen-
dants, or the living presence of human beings who were in contact
with an eternal and unchanging core of true wisdom, Gurdjieff
made many determined researches on his own and also joined a
group of 15 or 20 men and one woman, all committed to the quest
for hidden knowledge. They called themselves "Seekers of the

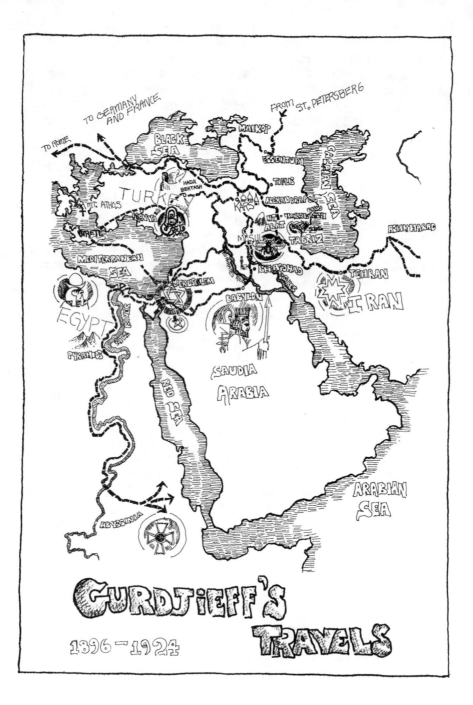

GURDJIEFF'S TRAVELS

1896-1924

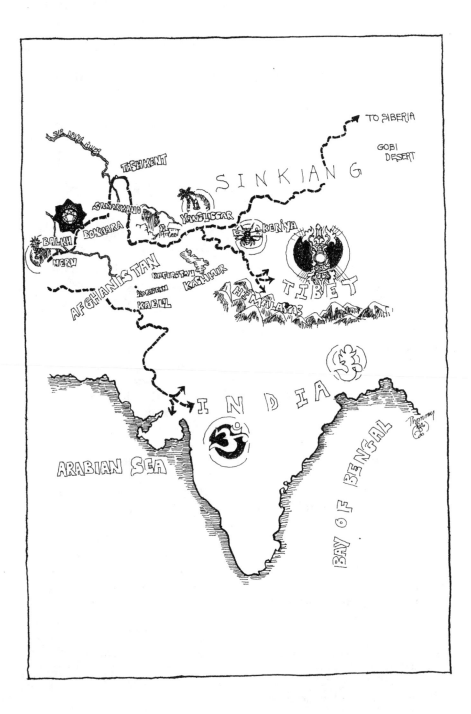

Truth." Travelling on major expeditions as a band, in twos and
threes, or occasionally alone, they combed the ruins of ancient civilizations in Egypt, Crete, Sumeria, Assyria and the Holy Land.
They visited monasteries and spiritual communities from Mount
Athos to Ethiopia and the Sudan. They traced the lineage of an
ancient brotherhood of wise men, the Sarmouni, through tekkias
of the Naqshbandi and Kadiri dervishes to the plains of Central
Asia. They even went all the way to the northern valleys of Siberia
in search of the shamanistic roots or offshoots of the knowledge
they sought.

"There were all kinds of specialists among us," Gurdjieff later
told one of his pupils. "Everyone studied on the lines of his particular subject. Afterwards, when we foregathered, we put together
everything we had found."[5] Gurdjieff was an expert hypnotist. He
was interested in the nature of suggestion. His main line of research
seems to have been the transformation of energy in the human
body, the states of consciousness possible for a human being and
the use of music, art, posture and gesture to modify consciousness.
He was deeply interested in ancient civilizations: Atlantis, pre-sand
Egypt, the great cities that once stood between the Tigris and
Euphrates, the birthplace of civilizations. The period in which he
travelled was a great archeological renaissance—Minos and Nineveh
and Babylon and Troy were just then being rediscovered. He sat
among the newly excavatêd ruins of Babylon, deeply absorbed in
psychic connection with those who knew and understood the
world in that ancient civilization. When he was in his twenties, the
Gilgamesh epic, familiar to him from childhood memories of his
father's recitations, was newly translated as the cuneiform script
in which it had been preserved was decoded.

The group uncovered evidence that in certain ancient civilizations there existed objective methods for composing melodies
which produced identical emotional responses in all listeners; build-
ings so constructed that altered states of consciousness were produced by merely walking into them, and dances so choreographed
that the inner state of the dancer was exactly determined. Gurdjieff collected dances. In them he hoped to find keys to the mys-
teries of the human body and mind.

Ceremonies and practices were also of significance as clues for
him.

"Every ceremony or rite has a value if it is performed without
alteration," he said. "A ceremony is a book in which a great deal
is written. Anyone who understands can read it. One rite often contains more than a hundred books."[6]

Yet perhaps the most profound influence on Gurdjieff's development came in his contacts with Sufism, the inward and essential subtlety behind the rituals of the Islamic world. He joined various orders and received dervish training, the most important contacts being in Afghanistan where he stayed for a long period in an isolated monastery in the Hindu Kush. He made a pilgrimage to Mecca and was disappointed: "If you want the truth, go to Bokhara," he told his followers. And Bokhara is the birthplace of the Naqshbandi order, whose founder, Bahaudin Naqshband, is referred to in Gurdjieff's writings as the Bokharan dervish Boggo-Eddin. The central symbol of the Gurdjieff work, the enneagram, is almost certainly of Sufi origin—an indication of the importance of these teachings in the system Gurdjieff developed.[7]

During his travels Gurdjieff was often without any means of support, it seems, and had to make his way by means of his own considerable native ingenuity. He traded carpets, remodelled corsets, retailed pickles, repaired anything and everything for a price, worked as a tourguide in the Holy City and around the Egyptian pyramids, set himself up as a hypnotist and magician—in short, made use of his already formidable powers of attention and suggestion to earn the money that allowed him to move like a gypsy from town to town. More than once he supplemented his native resourcefulness with a measure of charlatanism. On one occasion he peddled clipped and painted sparrows as rare "American canaries" and then skipped town before an untimely rain should wash away his deception. These business enterprises were quite successful in providing enough money to support Gurdjieff's quest for esoteric knowledge and were almost certainly also a cover for some additional activity as a political agent and spy.

Gurdjieff reports that he had "a propensity during this period for placing myself wherever there were revolutions, civil wars, social unrest, both to understand this sole aim of mine in a more concentrated form and to somehow discover some way for destroying the predilection which causes them (human beings) to fall so easily under the influence of mass hypnosis."[8] This propensity turned out to be hazardous for Gurdjieff who was, by his own report, hit on three different occasions by stray bullets, each time sustaining serious injuries that required long recuperation. On the first occasion, he was travelling in Crete in 1896, probably on an assignment from the Ethniki Etairea, a Russian-backed secret society organized to make political change in that part of the world.[9] Archeology was of great interest to Gurdjieff. His focus in the Cretan trip was probably in the Minoan ruins that had just begun to be unearthed

in the archeological digs of Sir Arthur Evans, and the Ethniki
Etairea with its Russian money was a convenient way to get to
Crete for an audacious young Caucasian on a shoestring.

The use of political events to further his own search for an
awakened inner circle of humanity was a running thread through
Gurdjieff's life. Bennett suggests that Gurdjieff's travels in search
of esoteric knowledge, in which he seems to have crossed a great
many national borders with peculiar ease, were facilitated by a
secret connection with the tsarist government. Louis Pauwels writes
in his book, *Gurdjieff*[10] :

> Gurdjieff was the principal Russian secret agent for ten years.
> (Kipling knew this.) He was given important financial posts by
> the Tibetan authorities and control over the equipment of the
> army. He was able to play a political role, as they knew him to
> possess spiritual powers and in this country that is all-important,
> especially among the high-ranking priesthood. He was tutor to the
> Dalai Lama, and escaped with him when the English invaded
> Tibet.

This account, from vague sources, is strongly disputed by some
of Gurdjieff's followers and seems historically unlikely if we piece together his own reports of his Tibetan journey, given in his last
work, *Life is Real Only Then, When "I Am."* What seems to have
happened is that the young Gurdjieff, whose aim it was to find a
lineage of enlightened masters and who also welcomed any chance
to observe social unrest and political tension as part of his study
of human behavior, was engaged by the Russian government to
conduct espionage activities in Tibet at a time when the Dalai
Lama asked for the Tsar's protection from British and Chinese
threats. Gurdjieff entered Tibet from the northwest at a time when
tension between Tibet and British-run governments to the south
made the Indian border virtually impassable. He probably made lib-
eral use of the similarity of his name to that of Lama Dorchieff,
tutor to the Dalai Lama, to gain entry into monasteries that might
otherwise have been inaccesssible to him.

Gurdjieff was looking for an awakened inner circle of humanity: the Tibetan tradition had an enduring esoteric circle in the re-
incarnate Rinpoche lamas. It is likely that he was able to make a
fruitful connection with the lineage, for much later in his life the
elderly Gurdjieff told how he used to wear red robes (as in the Tibetan tradition—other Buddhist monks wear ochre robes) with the
left shoulder exposed, in the company of many others similarly
dressed.

He was interested in dance and ritual movement. With his passable knowledge of spoken Tibetan he must have been able to learn something of the inner significance of certain sacred dances: he attributed many of the dances given by his pupils in European and American demonstrations decades later to sources in the Islamic world — but a few to sources within Tibet. He seems to have studied Buddhist theory and practice and to have received initiation and instruction in some aspects of energy control, since he reports that during the Tibetan period "by only a few hours of self-preparation I could from a distance of tens of miles kill a yak; or, in 24 hours, could accumulate life forces of such compactness that I could in five minutes put to sleep an elephant."[11]

It is not certain how long Gurdjieff continued his researches (and espionage) in Tibet, for all we know is that this period was brought to an abrupt end by another accident. Somehow, somewhere in Tibet, he was almost fatally wounded by a stray bullet. His companions managed to get him to Yanghissar in the Sinkiang Province to recuperate. There he spent several months unconscious, being nursed back to health by five physicians, three European and two Tibetan. During this time the British invaded Tibet and the Dalai Lama fled to China, then fled the Chinese to enter negotiations with the British in India, regaining a hold on his country only in 1912.

The third near-fatal accident, again caused by a stray bullet, occurred in the region of the Chiatur Tunnel in the Caucasus Mountains in 1904, during a time of civil disruption in which he was very likely engaged again in revolutionary activities and espionage. From this bullet wound he slowly recovered in various caves, making a tortuous journey back to Yanghissar to recuperate. During his convalescence he made an agonizing reassessment of the fruits of his studies: he had developed enormous powers, yet his mind and heart were full of associations that ran in the opposite direction from the ideals of his consciousness, and passions that demanded satisfaction. He felt the need for continuous attention that could be sustained in ordinary life and with which he could contact others. Yet he constantly forgot. No reminding factors helped him for long. Suddenly he was thunderstruck by a realization, a universal analogy:

> I am a man, and as such I am, in contrast to all other outer forms of animal life, created by Him in His image!!!
> For he is God and therefore I also have within myself all the possibilities and impossibilities that He has.
> The difference between Him and myself must lie only in scale.
> For He is God of all the presences in the universe! It follows that I also have to be God of some kind of presence on my scale.[12]

And yet, he reasoned, God had sent away from Himself one of His own, sent him into a condition of pride and given him a force equal and opposite to His own. How could this be? Could the same principle be used in microcosm, Gurdjieff mused? Then he knew:

> Thinking and thinking, I came to the conclusion that if I should intentionally stop utilizing the exceptional power in my possession which had been developed by me consciously in my own common life with people, then there must be forced out of me such a reminding source.
>
> Namely, the power based upon strength in the field of "handbledzoin" or, as it would be called by others, the power of telepathy and hypnotism.
>
> Thanks mainly to this inherency, developed in me by myself, I, in the process of general life, especially for the last two years, had been spoiled and depraved to the core, so that most likely this would remain all my life.
>
> And so, if consciously I would deprive myself of this grace of my inherency, then undoubtedly always and in everything its absence would be felt.
>
> I take an oath to remember never to make use of this inherency of mine and thereby to deprive myself from satisfying most of my vices. In the process of living together with others, this beloved inherency will always be a reminder for me.[13]

With this vow, from which he specifically excluded using his powers in the service of research, Gurdjieff felt "as if reincarnated." He may have then begun his mission to bring his understanding of the "terror of the situation" and of the possibility of a way out to the Western world.

THE RUSSIAN PERIOD

His entry into the Occident was via Russia. He must have spent some time at the court of Tsar Nicholas II, with its fascination for the occult, for he married a lady of the court, Countess Ostrofska, sometime during his Russian sojourn.

The next time Gurdjieff's whereabouts are certain is in 1915 when he was teaching groups in St. Petersburg and Moscow. There he found, or was found by Peter Ouspensky, the man who was to become Plato to his Socrates, as Colin Wilson put it in *The Outsider*.[14] Ouspensky had himself just returned from travels in search of genuine esoteric knowledge, and was amazed to find what he had been looking for was in his native land, and, in fact, in his hometown. He describes their first meeting in his book *In Search of the Miraculous* as follows:

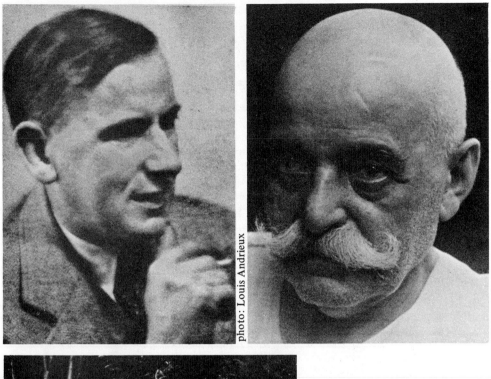

photo: Louis Andrieux

upper left: A.R. Orage
upper right: Gurdjieff
lower left: J.G. Bennett & wife
          (taken shortly before
          his death in December
          1974)

> I remember this meeting very well. We arrived at a small cafe
> in a noisy though not central street. I saw a man of an oriental
> type, no longer young, with a black moustache and piercing eyes,
> who astonished me first of all because he seemed to be disguised
> and completely out of keeping with the place and atmosphere. I
> was still full of impressions of the East. And this man with the
> face of an Indian raja or an Arab sheik whom I at once seemed to
> see in a white burnoose or a gilded turban, seated here in this little
> cafe, where small dealers and commission agents met together, in a
> black overcoat with a velvet collar and a black bowler hat, pro-
> duced the strange, unexpected and almost alarming impression of
> a man poorly disguised the sight of whom embarrasses you be-
> cause you see he is not what he pretends to be and yet you have
> to speak and behave as if you did not see it. He spoke Russian in-
> correctly with a strong Caucasian accent; and this accent, with
> which we are accustomed to associate anything apart from philo-
> sophical ideas, strengthened still further the strangeness and unex-
> pectedness of the impression.[15]

Ouspensky was impressed. Gurdjieff, alien as he still was to the
Westernized Russian mind, was presenting ideas in a way that rang true,
that threw new light on basic questions about man in relation to the
universe, levels of consciousness, the human condition, mortality
and immortality, and the possibility of self-realization—and he was
encouraging and even insisting upon personal verification. So Ouspensky joined a group of Gurdjieff followers who were meeting se-
cretly in Moscow and worked with them until the group disbanded
under the threat of revolution.

As Olga de Hartmann, one of his earliest Russian students, describes this period: "Russia in 1917 was torn by war and revolution. Mr. Gurdjieff was an unknown person, a mystery. Nobody
knew about his teaching, nobody knew his origin or why he had appeared in Moscow and St. Petersburg. But whoever came in contact
with him wished to follow him, and so did Thomas de Hartmann
and I."[16] So the de Hartmanns, Peter Ouspensky and his wife, and
a number of other students fled Russia, in a tortuous journey over
the mountains on foot, to Essentuki in the Caucasus, and when life
became impossible there, to Tiflis. Here Gurdjieff was joined by
other students, including Alexander and Jeanne de Salzmann from
Paris and together they began a new group that continued to work
under his guidance. Within a matter of months, however, the effects
of the revolution were felt in Tiflis, and Gurdjieff took his followers
to Constantinople, then to Berlin, and finally, after years of hard-
ship and refugee existence, to Paris. Here Gurdjieff decided to settle
and within a year gathered the money necessary to acquire the

Chateau of Avon, near Fontainebleau, where he founded the Institute for the Harmonious Development of Man.

GURDJIEFF IN EUROPE

The decade from 1922 to 1933 was spent in intense work with students at the Institute, during which time Gurdjieff tested and revised a system of study, self-observation, physical work, and exercise aimed toward the reconciliation and union of the three basic human functions of thinking, feeling, and physical activity. Many pupils came to stay at the Institute, including such notables as Katherine Mansfield (who died there), A.R. Orage, Maurice Nicoll, and the de Salzmanns. Gurdjieff, however, made no distinctions on the basis of eminence, and whoever came to study with him could be sure to be required to make consistent and intense efforts and also to be exposed to Gurdjieff's particular style of work on ego, which involved planned interpersonal friction and the public acknowledgment, if not actual ridicule, of personal patterns of malfunction. Every moment at the "Prieure," as the chateau was called, was regarded as an opportunity for developing self-awareness and attuning personal attitudes—from work in the gardens, to housebuilding, to cooking and cleaning as well as in the more formal instruction. Mealtimes were particularly likely to produce talk and teaching by Gurdjieff, who would often end a dinner with toasts to specific members of the group as various kinds of idiots—round idiots, square idiots, compassionate idiots, and nineteen other varieties. These celebrations of individual personality characteristics were part of the attempt, carried on by Gurdjieff on many fronts simultaneously, to invalidate and detoxify patterns of conditioning so that the student's essential nature could begin to appear.

This period of intense work included exhibitions and lectures in Europe and America. It was punctuated by a serious accident which occurred in 1925, soon after his return from his first American visit while Gurdjieff was driving alone in a small Citroen, and from which physicians were amazed to see him recover. He began, while still recuperating, to turn his attention to writing and eventually completed his three major works, which consist of ten books divided into three series. Of these the first series, *All and Everything*[17], and the second series, *Meetings with Remarkable Men*[18], are available. The third work, *Life is Real only Then, When "I Am"*[19], has been published privately in fragmentary form for those actively engaged in the Gurdjieff work.

These books deserve and, in fact, need some introduction. According to Gurdjieff[20], they are written to solve the following fundamental problems facing mankind:

> First Series: To destroy, mercilessly, without any compromises
> whatsoever, in the mentation and feelings of the reader, the be-
> liefs and views, by centuries rooted in him, about everything ex-
> isting in the world.
>   Second Series: To acquaint the reader with the material re-
> quired for a new creation and to prove the soundness and good
> quality of it.
>   Third Series: To assist the arising, in the mentation and the
> feelings of the reader, of a veritable, nonfantastic representation
> not of that illusory world which he now perceives, but of the
> world existing in reality.

The first series concerns the "three-brained beings"—mankind
—on planet earth as described by Beelzebub to his grandson Has-
sein as they travel in the spaceship Karnak. Beelzebub recounts
what he saw and learned about humanity during his six visits to
this unhappy planet, how the inhabitants function and how they
could function, what has been done by cosmic forces to provide
aid, and how the situation has continued to deteriorate. The mag-
num opus of Gurdjieff's life, this work is an encyclopedic commen-
tary on the most urgent questions facing every individual. It is difficult to read in part because, in his wish to avoid words that had
incorrect connotations and past associations (or perhaps in order
to require an additional committed effort on the part of the reader)
Gurdjieff has chosen to introduce new vocabulary, including words
such as Heptaparaparshinokh (roughly translated as "sevenfold-
ness"), Hanbledzoin ("that substance that arises in the common
presence of a man from all intentionally made being-efforts") and
even Tescooano (telescope). The serious reading of this book is virtually guaranteed by the use of this new and unfamiliar vocabulary.
Students of the work will be aided by a concordance prepared re-
cently by a Gurdjieff group.[21]

The second series appears to be very easily penetrable and is
as enjoyable as a good adventure story. It seems to tell the story of
Gurdjieff's early years, his first tutors, and the extraordinary individuals he met on his journeys in search of esoteric knowledge, but
actually includes a good deal of teaching material and allegory.

The third series is much more direct than its antecedents. It gives
an account of Gurdjieff's personal development and describes specific
practices which develop attention and awareness of self; thus, like
the oral tradition in any spiritual technology, it is reserved for those
who have left idle curiosity behind.

In addition to these works, Gurdjieff wrote and distributed

another, smaller book, *The Herald of the Coming Good*,[22] in which he introduced the ideas on which his work rests, described the Institute for the Harmonious Development of Man, and announced the forthcoming publication of the first and second series. This book was the only one published during his lifetime.

THE LATER YEARS

The years between 1933 and 1949, when he died in Paris, marked a new phase of Gurdjieff's activity in which he closed the Prieure and traveled widely, starting new groups in several American cities. At the time of his death he may have had several hundred pupils, mainly in New York and Paris. Ouspensky had broken sharply with him and had died before him, leaving a group of students committed to Ouspensky's version of the work in London. Gurdjieff's writings were practically unknown, and his influence on European thought and culture, apart from the deep impressions made on his pupils, was virtually nil.

Yet now the students of his teachings number in the thousands. His name day is ritually celebrated on January 13, with festivities, music, sacred dances; and the anniversary of his death, October 29, is honored with Russian orthodox memorial services. The ideas Gurdjieff offered to the Western world continue to ring true. The growth of his influence must be due, at least in some measure, to the current resurgence of interest in self-realization that has led those suffering from what Jung called "holy neurosis" to seek out spiritual guidance wherever it is authentically present. In part, however, it must be due to the fact that Gurdjieff was successful, at least in a considerable degree, in the effort he made to translate esoteric methods and ideas related to the unfolding of man into terms that were specifically evocative for contemporary Westerners. Whether he was "the first emmissary to the West" from a great Middle Eastern teaching school, as he has been called by some, or whether he was working under his own auspices, his efforts merit the consideration of post-industrial seekers after truth who, tired of what the material world, the world of business and even the world of academia can offer, turn inward to seek reality.

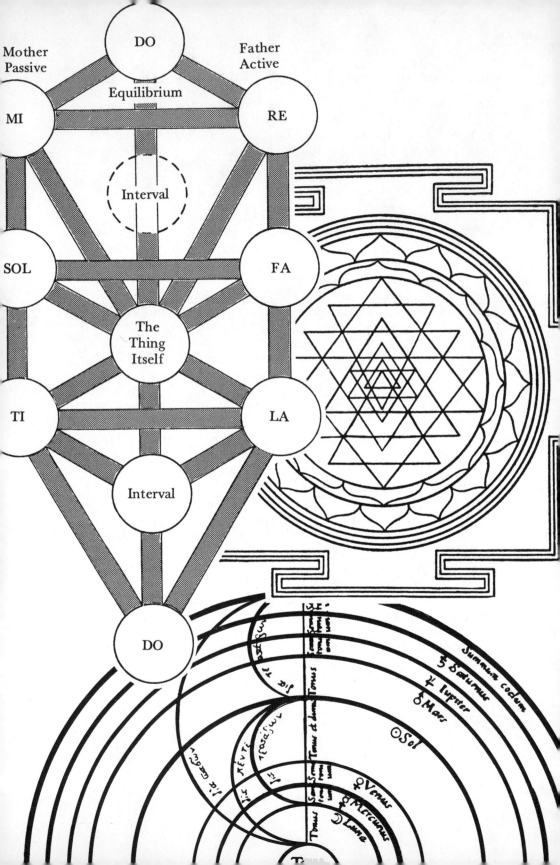

CHAPTER TWO:
The Philosophical Basis of Gurdjieff's System

According to Gurdjieff, we live in a very poor place in the universe, from the point of view of our possible evolution. Self-realization is almost maximally difficult owing to the extreme density of mechanical laws that operate on our planet so that, although human beings are designed, so to speak, with the potential for increasing the level of their being, the chance that any particular individual will succeed in doing so is very slim. Because of the factors operating against one, a person must expect that inner growth will not be easy: on the contrary, it will require great understanding and skillful effort, and this effort can begin only when one realizes the truth about the human condition. Plato likened the human being to someone fascinated by the shadows dancing on the rear wall of a cave, who is so engrossed that he is heedless of the world behind him. Gurdjieff compares the "normal" human state to that of a prisoner:

> You do not realize your own situation. You are in prison. All you can wish for, if you are a sensible man, is to escape. But how escape? It is necessary to tunnel under a wall. One man can do nothing. But let us suppose there are ten or twenty men—if they work in turn and if one covers another they can complete the tunnel and escape.
>
> Furthermore, no one can escape from prison without the help of those *who have escaped before*. Only they can say in what way escape is possible or can send tools, files, or whatever may be necessary. But *one* prisoner alone cannot find these people or get in touch with them. An organization is necessary. Nothing can be achieved without an organization.[1]

Liberation, then, depends first upon the realization of the truth about our condition. Once this understanding has hit home, it is not enough to be very intelligent or very highly motivated to do something about it: precise instructions, maps, and knowledge are needed by those who have already liberated themselves, and these "tools" must be used cooperatively.

One of the obstacles facing those who seek to liberate themselves is that humanity exists on this planet for a definite purpose, and that purpose would not be served if more than a certain percentage of people attained extraordinary levels of being—in fact, the flow of substances from the highest levels to the lowest would be severely disrupted if mankind's general level of consciousness were to change. The biosphere serves as an energy transducer at a critical place in a constantly evolving universe, serving to bridge the gap between sun and solar system and our own moon.

In order to understand this fact about the human situation we must look at our place in the cosmos, conceived by Gurdjieff as orderly emanations from a creative center in a system strongly reminiscent of Plotinus and Ibn al-Arabi. We will designate the prime mover, or origin, the Absolute. Out of the Absolute proceeds a very great number, perhaps an infinite number, of *Rays of Creation*. Looking down one of these (the one that interests us most, namely our own), we see that out of the Absolute emanate all possible systems or worlds, and from all worlds come all suns, our sun, the planets in our solar system, our planet, the earth, and finally the moon. These steps in the Ray of Creation differ in the number of laws under which they operate. At the level of the Absolute there is only one law, the unity of the will of creation; in the next world there are three orders of laws; in the next, six; in the next, twelve. On our earth there are 48 orders of laws under which we must live. The only place on the Ray of Creation in which it would be more difficult to strive for liberation would be the moon, which is governed by 96 orders of laws.

THE RAY OF CREATION

Absolute	①	
World 3 under 3 laws	③	All Possible Systems of Worlds
World 6 under 6 laws	⑥	The Milky Way
World 12 under 12 laws	⑫	The Sun
World 24 under 24 laws	㉔	The Planets as One Mass
World 48 under 48 laws	㊽	The Earth
World 96 under 96 laws	�996	The Moon

The will of the Absolute is manifest only on the level of all worlds, which it creates directly. The plan or pattern created at that level proceeds mechanically, level after level, until it reaches the very end of the Ray of Creation which is, in our case, the moon. Because we live under 48 laws we are very far from the will of the Absolute. If we could free ourselves from half of those laws we would be one step closer, and if we could free ourselves from half of *those* laws we would be one step closer, and if we could reduce the number of laws we live under to only twelve we would be still closer. Moving toward the Absolute by liberating oneself, stage by stage, from the mechanical laws constraining us is the path of self-realization.

Everything in the universe is weighable and measurable, although the matter from which everything is made exists in differing degrees of density. The seven steps in the Ray of Creation may be thought of as the seven levels or orders of materiality, each differing in the rate of vibration: the Absolute vibrates most rapidly and is least dense, and the levels below it become more dense and slower in rate of vibration until the moon, the slowest and densest place on our ray, is reached. Of these orders of matter the finer permeate the denser and coarser ones. Thus everything around us and familiar to us is in fact permeated with all the levels of matter that exist, including the Absolute.

> There is no need to study or investigate the sun in order to discover the matter of the solar world: this matter exists in ourselves and is the result of the division of our atoms. In the same way we have in us the matter of all other worlds. Man is, in the full sense of the term, a "miniature universe"; in him are all the matters of which the universe consists; the same forces, the same laws that govern the life of the universe, operate in him; therefore in studying man we can study the whole world, just as in studying the world we can study man.[2]

Of these universal laws the most basic, perhaps, since it applies to every event, everywhere, is called by Gurdjieff the Law of Three. This law states that every manifestation is the resultant of three forces, which may be called active, passive, and neutralizing or Holy Affirming, Holy Denying, and Holy Neutralizing or, more simply, first force, second force, and third force. These forces, like the *gunas* of Vedanta, are present everywhere, even in the very first step of the ray of creation, where they are unified, as reflected in many of the world's religions as Brahma, Vishnu, and Shiva; Father, Son, and Holy Spirit, and other trinities.

> Every action is really performed by the *gunas*. Man, deluded by

his egoism, thinks: "I am the doer." But he who has the true insight into the operations of the gunas and their various functions, knows that when senses attach themselves to objects, *gunas* are merely attaching themselves to *gunas*.[3]

Creation depends on the conjunction of these three forces: nothing can take place unless all three are present. Without neutralizing force, active and passive forces stand in useless opposition and nothing new can emerge, but when this third force is present, active and passive forces can join and produce results. We in our present state of consciousness are blind to third force: it requires a higher level of awareness than the ordinary state to see more than duality in things. But there are a few examples that may be readily pointed out in the sciences, such as the action of catalysts in chemistry, for purposes of illustration.

THE LAW OF THREE: EXAMPLES[4]

	FIRST FORCE [POSITIVE]	SECOND FORCE [NEGATIVE]	THIRD FORCE [NEUTRALIZING]	TOTAL PHENOMENON
Physics	nucleus (neutrons, etc.)	electrons	electromagnetic field	atom
Engineering	architectural decision and planning	construction work	geographical site	city
Law	plaintiff	defendant	judge	settlement of dispute
Biology	thermo-dynamic energies	chemical entities	electro-dynamic organic field	biological organism
Psychology	experiential content (e.g. the color blue, anger, introspection)	neurological functioning (sensory, basal gangliar and cerebro-integrative processes)	conscious entity (whose transforming mediation is consciousness or pure awareness)	human being

When the three forces do meet and an act of creation takes place, a chain of manifestations may develop in which third force in one event becomes active force in the next event—for the three forces change sign with respect to one another as they go about spinning or braiding the thread of occurrences. Now the second fundamental law, the Law of Seven, begins to operate.

The Law of Seven governs successions of events. It states that whenever any manifestation evolves, it does so nonlinearly. There is an orderly discontinuity in every progression of things, in every series. This lawful discontinuity is preserved in our musical scale which, as singing up and down any octave will show, is composed of

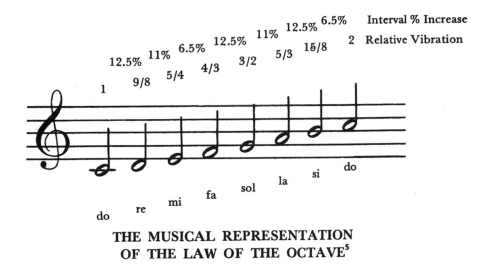

**THE MUSICAL REPRESENTATION
OF THE LAW OF THE OCTAVE**[5]

unequal steps. Do, re, and mi are equally distant from one another, but between mi and fa there is a half-step instead of a full step. Proceeding up the scale, we have sol, la, and si (ti in some usages) separated by full intervals, but si and do having a half-step between them again.

The Law of Seven explains why when something begins it does not just continue and continue, *ad infinitum:* why a rainstorm abates or a grudge finally loses its venom. And the Law of Seven is behind the fact that there are no straight lines in nature. It is also reflected in the Ray of Creation.

If we redraw the Ray of Creation so that it is a descending octive going from the level of the Absolute to the level of the moon, the discontinuities appear between the Absolute and the level of all worlds, and between all planets and the earth. The first of these gaps or discontinuities is bridged by the force of creation engendered by the Absolute itself. The second requires our biosphere: the sensitive living film of organic life on earth acts as a transmitter of energy between the planetary level of the Ray of creation and our own planet and its satellite moon, the lower part of the ray.

THE RAY OF CREATION AS AN OCTAVE

Level of the Absolute	①	Do	
			SHOCK
Level of All Possible Systems of Worlds	③	Si	
Level of Our Milky Way	⑥	La	
Level of Our Sun	⑫	Sol	
Level of Planets	㉔	Fa	
			SHOCK
Level of Our Earth	㊽	Mi	
Level of Our Moon	(96)	Re	

The Law of Seven may also be called the law of shock, for if an additional force or energy enters a process between mi and fa it will proceed on course until the si—do interval, and if another shock or influx of energy is given at that point the process continues to its conclusion at do. In the Ray of Creation this energy is generated by mankind and other living things. In this sense we ex-

---

THE LAW OF SEVEN IN EVERYDAY LIFE: THE OCTAVE OF MAKING THIS BOOK

	Do	Idea of book
Shock [Decision to Proceed]	□	
	Si	All Possible forms of book
	La	Particular type of book
	Sol	Specific requirements and characteristics
	Fa	Detailed plan
Shock [Materials and skill]	□	
	Mi	Preparation of manuscript
	Re	Printing and publication
	Do	Actual published book

ist to serve nature and it is not in the interest of nature that humanity be anything more than an energy transducer coating the planet.
In another perspective, mankind is created incomplete and has the
possibility of evolving to the level of the sun—World 12—or even
further, and there are forces striving to complete an ascending octave in every human being, forces that go astray for want of specific additional energies skillfully applied.

The octave relationships in the Law of Seven exist in all processes, according to Gurdjieff. Seeing them is a matter of arraying
whatever is to be studied appropriately or finding the right metric.
In chemistry there is a very clear example in the periodic table of
elements in which the essential characteristics of chemical elements
are seen to repeat themselves every eighth element when they are
ordered according to atomic weight. It is, however, unnecessary to
search very far for examples of octave relationships since they are
present in every project we undertake, from cooking a meal to
building a house.

The union of the Law of Three and the Law of Seven is represented in a diagram, much like the Kabbalistic Tree of Life, that is
central in Gurdjieff's teaching—the enneagram. The enneagram is a
circle divided into nine equal parts. Numbering the points by moving around the circumference clockwise, we can then form a triangle by connecting points 9, 6 and 3. This triangle represents the
trinity or Law of Three. If we think of the whole of creation as
manifestation seeking to be reabsorbed into the Absolute unity
we can see how the three perpetuates itself: three tries to return
to the One; that is, in mathematical terms, 3 into 1, $1 \div 3$, which
produces a recurring series, .333333 . . . The other points around
the circle are connected in a way that reflects the tendency for
manifestation according to the Law of Seven to return to unity:
7 into 1, $1 \div 7 = .142857142857142$, etc., a recurring series of six
digits containing no multiple of three. Thus both great laws are
represented on one symmetrical diagram in a way that reflects their
complementariness and interrelationship.

The enneagram can be used in the study of all processes since
it must be present in all sequences of events. The days of the week
can, for example, be laid out around the circumference. Now we
see all sorts of intriguing possibilities. Sunday is at the point where
the trinity enters the week as is reflected in the Christian Sabbath.
Shock points seem to occur on Tuesday and Thursday nights. And
there seem to be two progressions in the week: the sequence of
chronological time is represented on the outer circle while some

THE ENNEAGRAM

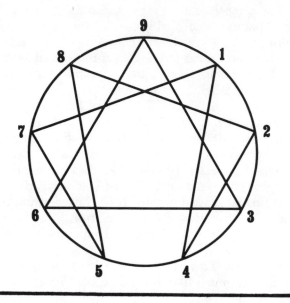

other sequence, a flow from Monday to Wednesday and back to
Tuesday, from Tuesday to Saturday and then to Thursday and to
Friday, is represented by the inner connecting lines. Some non-
obvious inner relationship between days is indicated: synchronici-
ties begin to make sense. Something that I do (or am about to do,
if you want to think linearly) on Wednesday may affect what I experience on Tuesday. Extending this idea we can consider the possibility that there are connections between events outside the chronological progression of cause and effect that might, for instance,
modify today's pattern of happenings to account for a future cala-
mity or victory. This idea is very close to the Buddhist doctrine of
multiple causation and to Heisenberg's startling principle of uncertainty.

From the point of view of the transformation of oneself from
what is—in religious traditions—seen as the fallen condition into
the state of perfection there is much wisdom within the enneagram. We are what we eat. Ordinarily, the transformation of food
in the human body is accomplished with the shock of air coming
between mi and fa in the octave that goes from what is taken into
the mouth to what is actually used by the body. The influx of air
both furthers the assimilation of food and begins a new octave. It

ENNEAGRAM OF DAYS OF THE WEEK

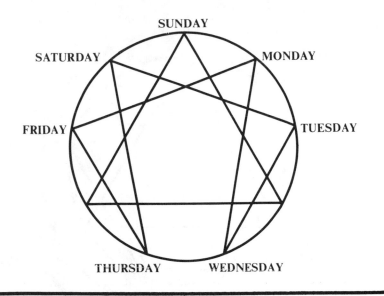

is a shock that is delivered to all sentient beings with every breath.

Air can also be assimilated. Each breath both furthers the digestion of food and begins a new octave which usually gets no further than mi because it does not receive the shock necessary for it to pass into fa. If this shock were given it would initiate a new octave of the assimilation of impressions which would also require a shock to pass into its fa. These shocks are not delivered automatically. To assimilate air, according to Gurdjieff, one must give oneself what is called the *first conscious shock* by receiving impressions consciously, by remembering oneself. Then to assimilate impressions and complete the "eating" possible for human beings one must give the *second conscious shock* which involves the transmutation of negative emotional energy produced by external circumstances. These higher shocks involve increased awareness: the first conscious shock is a mindful witnessing of whatever is happening while the second conscious shock requires that subtle inner processes be adroitly redirected.

If we fully metabolized the food, air and impressions we receive we would live to the fullest, but as we ordinarily live only the assimilation of food is carried out properly. The assimilation of breath is halted and its octave stopped, for lack of a shock at its

ENNEAGRAM OF TRANSFORMATION OF FOOD[6]

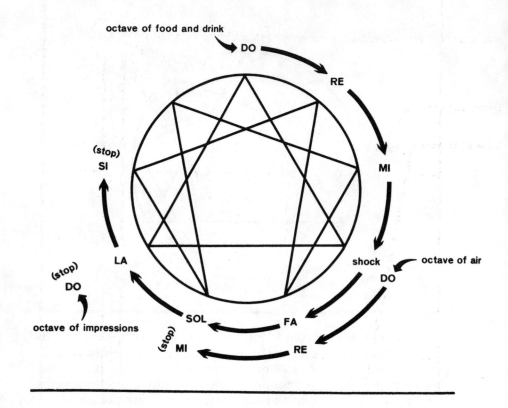

octave of food and drink

DO

RE

(stop)
SI

MI

LA

shock   octave of air
DO

(stop)
DO

SOL   FA

octave of impressions

(stop)
MI   RE

---

mi—fa interval, and the octave of assimilation of impressions, the
nourishment most vital to life, is aborted at its very inception. With
skillful means these octaves can be brought to completion. It is
with the production and absorption of these shocks that all esoteric teaching is technically concerned.

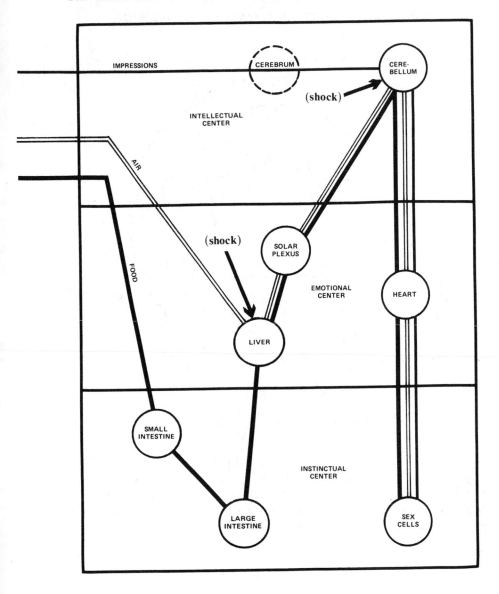

WHAT SELF-OBSERVATION DOES TO THE BODY
Digestion After the First Conscious Shock

It is possible to get out of a trap. However, in order to break out of a prison, one first must confess to being in a prison. The trap is man's emotional structure, his character structure. There is little use in devising systems of thought about the nature of the trap if the only thing to do in order to get out of the trap is to know the trap and to find the exit.

—Wilhelm Reich

For my part, when I enter most intimately into what I call myself, *I always stumble on some particular perception or other, of heat or cold, light or shade, love or hatred, pain or pleasure. I never catch* myself *at any time without a perception, and never can observe anything but the perception . . . I may venture to affirm [that human beings are] nothing but a bundle or collection of different perceptions, which succeed each other with inconceivable rapidity, and are in a perpetual flux and movement.*

—David Hume

I think the main objection to behaviorism is that people are in love with the mental apparatus. If you say that doesn't really exist, that it's a fiction and let's get back to the facts, then they have to give up their first love.

—B.F. Skinner

CHAPTER THREE

The Psychology of Ordinary Human Beings

It will be convenient, in studying Gurdjieff's teachings about human psychology, to look at the issues from two points of view: our condition as it is now, and our condition as it would be if we were to realize our possibilities, our destiny, to the fullest.

HUMAN FRAGMENTATION

The human condition, as made manifest in almost every one of us, is, according to Gurdjieff, substantially different from our ordinary notions of it. This difference between how one thinks one is and how one is in actuality is most strikingly evident with respect to notions about personal identity, responsible action and free will, though it applies with equal validity to hosts of other, lesser, human functions as well. Take, for example, the idea we all have deeply ingrained in us that each of us is one consistent person. It is generally accepted by students of personality and by practically everyone else also that except in cases of hysterical dissociation, which are very rare, when a person says "I" he or she refers to himself in his entirety. And each person who says "I" assumes that he or she speaks as an entity that persists hour after hour, day after day. That is how we represent ourselves to others and what we generally accept as a self-evident truth. After all, each individual has one familiar body that is a consistent factor in daily experience. Ouspensky says:

> The illusion of unity or oneness is created in man first, by the sensation of one physical body, *by his name*, which in normal cases always remains the same, and third, by a number of mechanical habits which are implanted in him by education or acquired by imitation. Having always the same physical sensations, hearing always the same name and noticing in himself the same habits and inclinations he had before, he believes himself to be always the same.[1]

It may be, however, that human psychological structure and function are better explained by looking at behavior in terms of many
"I's" rather than one, a concept of self more akin to the Buddhist
view than to Western psychological thought (although even in the
West there has been a thread of this sort of thinking, one that has
influenced contemporaries as diverse as Assagioli[2] and Skinner[3]).
According to Gurdjieff each adult has many selves, each of which
uses the word "I" to describe itself. At one moment one "I" is
present and at another there is a different "I" who may or may not
be in sympathy with the previous "I." This "I" may not even know
the other "I" exists for between "I's" there are often relatively im-
penetrable defenses called *buffers*. Clusters of "I's" make up sub-
personalities that are related by association; some for business,
others for family, others for the church or synagogue. These clusters may not know other clusters of "I's" with which they are not
related by association. One "I" may promise and another may
have no knowledge of the promise, owing to buffers, and therefore
no intention of honoring it. One group of "I's" may rush enthusi-
astically into a marriage that makes others resentful and withdrawn.
Certain "I's" may value and work toward an aim that others sub-
vert, and one may suffer "the nature of insurrection." Seen from
Gurdjieff's perspective, then, psychotherapeutic techniques that
bring the various fragments of ego into awareness—from the basic
rule of psychoanalysis to the explicit inner dialogues of Gestalt—
would have the important function of gradually reducing the effects of buffers and acquainting the "I's" with one another.

THE HUMAN MACHINE

Not only is human psychological functioning characterized by
inconsistency, but this inconsistency is entirely determined by
mechanical laws. The "I" that is in control of a person's behavior
at any given moment is determined not by his or her personal
choice but by a reaction to the surrounding environment which
evokes one or another "I." The human being cannot choose which
"I" to be, much as one would like to: the situation chooses. Our
behavior is elicited, not emitted, and what happens to us occurs
entirely because of external influences and the "accidental" associations of conditioning history. We have no capacity to do, no
"free will"—in fact, no function of will at all. Attractions and aversions, tendencies to approach or avoid whatever stimuli impinge
on a person act as invisible strings that animate the marionette
that he or she is. In Gurdjieff's words:

> Man is a machine. All his deeds, actions, words, thoughts, feelings,

> convictions, opinions and habits are the result of external influ-
> ences, external impressions. Out of himself a man cannot produce
> a single thought, a single action. Everything he says, does, thinks,
> feels—all this happens.... Man is born, lives, dies, builds houses,
> writes books, not as he wants to, but as it happens. Everything hap-
> pens. Man does not love, hate, desire—all this happens.[4]

In the undeveloped state which is our common lot the human being is, then, like a very complex and intricate machine that unlike
other machines has the potentiality of knowing it is a machine. The
human "machine" can study itself. This study may yield the clues
necessary to attain another, higher level of being in which true will
is possible. But this study, like the study of any other complex system, may take a long time and require much persistence and attention.

OUR THREE "BRAINS"

In Gurdjieff's *All and Everything*, Beelzebub tells his grandson all about the "inexplicable behavior of those three-brained beings on that strange planet Earth." These three brains correspond,
like stories in a building (and in particular, a food factory), to
three distinct levels of function. The upper story is the intellectual
center, the middle story contains the emotional center, and the
lower story is the locus of control for three functions which sometimes work independently but often do not. These are the moving
center, the instinctive center, and the sexual center. In addition to
these five centers, which are operative in every normal person, there
are two more centers which, although they are perfectly formed
and always functioning, have no connection to the others unless
one is intentionally and skillfully made. These are the higher intellectual center (whose language is symbol) in the top story and the
higher emotional center (whose language is myth) in the middle story.
In ordinary people the five lower centers function inefficiently and out of harmony with one another and the higher centers are
not used. The lower centers use different forms of energy, yet they
borrow and steal energy from one another even though it cannot
be properly used. They waste virtually all the energy they have at
their disposal in leaks that are so chronic and so debilitating that
unless measures are taken to stop them there is no way to sustain
a raised level of functioning of centers at all. And they habitually
perform functions that are not their own, interfering with one another and degrading the work output. All the centers habitually rob
sex center of its energy, which is of a higher vibrational level than
that used by the other centers and therefore not necessary for their

The three centers in a human being correspond to three distinct levels of function: intellectual, emotional, instinctual.

THE CENTERS

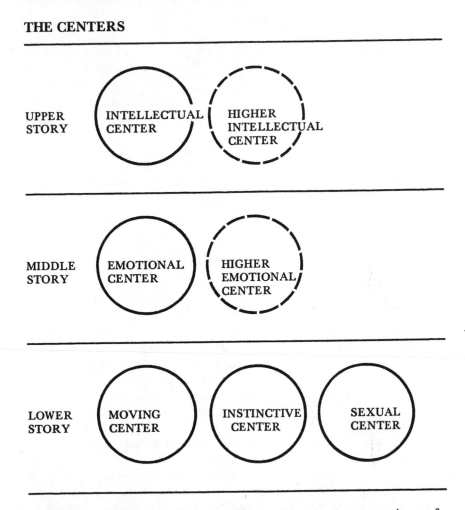

proper functioning. This finer energy leaks away in expressions of fanaticism, vehemence, and misplaced enthusiasm while sex center, like a racing car filled with low octane fuel, works with inferior energy and virtually never functions to its fullest capacity.

Other centers, too, do not work at nearly their full potential. If the emotional center were operating to the fullest it would become connected with the higher emotional center and if the intellectual center were operating correctly it, too, would become connected with the higher center corresponding to it. These connections require a match in vibrational levels between lower and higher centers. Permanent connections with the higher centers can, therefore, be forged only when the work of the lower centers has been

MISUSES OF SEXUAL ENERGY

INTELLECTUAL CENTER	disputes
	criticism
	polemic
	battles with words
	sexual fantasy and
	satisfaction by such fantasy
EMOTIONAL CENTER	preaching hellfire and
	damnation, the horror of
	sin, eternal pain
	religious persecution
	sentimentality
	jealousy
	cruelty
MOVING CENTER	making sports records
	climbing mountains
	"just because they're there"

(The misuse of sexual energy is identified by a particular vehemence in the act and the uselessness of the work produced.)

---

regulated and quickened. Temporary connections do occur spontaneously in ecstatic moments, but these must be brief until the lower centers are prepared for the energy flow involved. As we are, we could no more tolerate such connections than, say, an appliance designed for 110 volts could stand connection with a 220-volt power supply.

Not only do the lower centers function below their capacity, waste energy, rob and steal from each other, and function unharmoniously with respect to one another in a host of ways, but even within centers there is a misapplication of effort. Each center is divided into intellectual, emotional, and moving parts, and each of these parts typically (though not always) has a positive and negative aspect, and is further subdivided into intellectual, emotional, and moving aspects. As an example of the wrong work of intellectual center, Nicoll gives the following:

> The mechanical part includes in itself all the work of registration of *memories, associations, and impressions,* and this is all the work it should do normally—that is, when the other centers and parts of centers are doing *their* proper work. It should only do the work of registration or recording, like a secretary taking down what is said and arranging it, etc. And, as was said, it should never reply to questions addressed to the *whole center* and should never decide anything important: but unfortunately it is always

deciding and always replying in its narrow limited way, with ready-made phrases, and it continues to say the same things and work in the same mechanical way under all conditions.[5]

THE FUNCTIONS OF CENTERS[6]

	MOVING PART	EMOTIONAL PART	INTELLECTUAL PART
MOVING CENTER	Automatic reflexes Imitation on small scale Limited adaptability to learning new movements	Pleasure in movement Normal love of games Higher imitation: some forms of acting	Inventing things and machines Making adaptations
INSTINCTIVE CENTER	Pleasant sensations Unpleasant sensations	Blind animal love "Instinctive" love Animal jealousy Animal rage: desire to kill	Many so-called intuitions
SEXUAL CENTER	Sexual sensations (can only be pleasant or neutral)	Sexual attraction and gratification or frustration feelings	Assumptions about sex Perceptions of sex
EMOTIONAL CENTER	Mechanical expression of emotions All emotions relating to one's likes and dislikes: personal emotions Small desires: little daily "wills"	Religious emotions Aesthetic emotions Moral emotions: may lead to conscience	Artistic creation Chief seat of magnetic center
INTELLECTUAL CENTER	Repetition of words and phrases: mechanical talking Inquisitiveness; curiosity Shrewdness; craftiness	Desire to know and understand, search for knowledge; higher kinds of imagination	Intellectual construction Creative thought Discovery

This part of intellectual center has been given a special name: formatory center or formatory apparatus. When it usurps the work of the entire intellectual center what results is "formatory thinking," characterized by stock phrases and slogans, and black-white, wrong-right, either-or comparisons that lack the depth and subtlety of intellectual thought.

The study of wrong work of centers is one of the keys to understanding the mechanics of human psychology. Some approximate descriptions of correct functions are summarized in the table (modified from Nicoll) to give a wider, though still incomplete, perspective.

Man's three stories have separate memory banks, each of which records impressions appropriate to it. Gurdjieff describes the mechanism of memory as follows:

> In a newly-born child these three diverse parts of the general human psyche may be compared to a system of blank gramophone rolls upon which begin to be recorded, from the day of its appearance into the world, the external significance of objects and the subjective understanding of their inner significance, or the sense of the results of all actions taking place in the outer world, as well as the inner world already forming in him: all this is recorded in accordance with the correspondence between the nature of these actions and the nature of the distinct systems which form themselves in man.
>
> All kinds of these recorded results of environing actions remain unchanged on each of these "depository rolls" for life, in the same sequence and in the same correlation with the impressions previously recorded, in which they are perceived.[7]

Theoretically, according to Gurdjieff, impressions can impinge upon an individual in different ways: they can come from mechanical associations or completely unconscious sensation of the world; they can come from voluntarily received impressions, active thinking, and conscious feeling; or they can come from a higher state of direct and conscious perception which is only a remote possibility for ordinary man, depending on how many shocks are received. As consciousness changes in level, the quality of impressions received changes as well. Most of life is spent in a dulled state of consciousness that is our ordinary waking state, and which we will discuss in more detail below. At this point it is sufficient to say that, in this state, impressions are related only by the mechanical laws of association, and it is thus that they are recorded by the centers. Consciousness varies in level, however: people bob up and down from level to level, sometimes more, sometimes less submerged in identification with actions and events in their experience. There are, occasionally, moments of higher states of consciousness. At these times, memory is quite different. It is far more vivid and immediate.

THREE HUMAN TYPES

The relative importance in an individual's patterns of functioning of each of the three stories of his "food factory" determines his or her place in a scheme of classification used by Gurdjieff to characterize human beings. One person may depend more on head than heart, for example, while another may allow emotion to hold

The three basic human types observed by Gurdjieff. They differ from one another in their habits, tastes, and styles of life.

sway over him where logic fails. Everyone is born with one "brain" predisposed to predominate over the other two. According to Gurdjieff's scheme, Man Number One has his center of gravity in moving and instinctive functions, Man Number Two gives more weight to feelings, and Man Number Three bases actions on knowledge or theoretical perspective. These individuals are more or less on the same level of being, since they all lack inner unity and will. They differ, however, in their reliance on one function or another.

Men Numbers One, Two, and Three differ from one another in their habits, tastes, and styles of life. They correspond roughly to Sheldon's varieties of physique.[8] Man Number One is endomorphic; Man Number Two, mesomorphic; and Man Number Three, ectomorphic. These body types are correlated with the temperamental constellations of visceratonia (emphasis on the gut, the instinct), somatotonia (emphasis on impulse and action) and cerebrotonia (emphasis on thinking) in Sheldon's system, which proves to be a very good fit for Gurdjieff's. In literary terms we can see them as three familiar Shakespearean characters: Falstaff is Man Number One; Prince Hal, Man Number Two; and Hamlet, Man Number Three.

For each of these three basic types there is a form of art, a form of music, a kind of religious practice that is most appealing. Man Number One is moved by pomp and ceremony, by sacred rites and holy repetitions, while Man Number Two has an affinity for prayer and devoted sacrifice before god or guru. Man Number Three theologizes, categorizes, debates and disputes in his almost tropistic orientation toward wisdom. The great religious traditions can accommodate all these types: consider the ponderous high masses of Catholicism, the fervent sermons of the evangelistic

THE THREE TYPES OF HUMAN BEINGS

Man Number One	Man Number Two	Man Number Three
Moving/Instinctive Man	Emotional Man	Thinking Man
Rote memorization and imitative learning	Knowledge of likes and dislikes	Logical thinking and literal interpretations
Primtive, sensual art	Sentimental art	Intellectual, invented art
Religion of rites and ceremonies	Religion of faith and love, and of persecution of heresy	Religion of proofs and arguments
Fakirs	Monks	Yogis
Karma yoga	Bhakti yoga	Jnana yoga

sects with their choruses of "Amens," the reasoned arguments of the Protestants. In Hinduism, Buddhism, Islam, Judaism there is similar scope for the spectrum of human affinities, for within the pattern of thoughts, feelings and actions of each sleeping being— lying precisely where there is most possible distortion—is the key to another way of living.

STATES OF CONSCIOUSNESS

In his ordinary state of awareness, an individual, whether type One, Two, or Three, does not pay attention to himself the way one likes to think one does. Awareness of moving, emotional, and intellectual functions is consciousness, and this consciousness is very hazy and inconsistent, very much below capacity. Any person, chosen at random in a business office, social club, or university lecture hall and imperceptibly followed throughout a normal day's routine by an acute observer, would be seen to be very seldom aware of who and where he or she is, and even more rarely to register on what he or she knows and does not know.

Gurdjieff distinguishes between four states of consciousness that are possible for human beings: sleep, ordinary waking state, self-consciousness, and objective consciousness. Although all these states are possible for each individual, they differ widely in duration and in probability of occurrence. Typically life is divided between sleep and ordinary waking state (which may be thought of as a form of sleep). In sleep we may spend a third or even more of our time on earth. This is because we sleep inefficiently: actually it does not take very long for the body to make the substances for which sleep was intended, according to Gurdjieff. The reason that ordinary people need so much time for sleep is that they spend most of it in transitional states between sleep and waking, states which are neither one nor the other and are unprofitable. These transitional states are characterized by dreams:

> Deep sleep is a state when we have no dreams or sensations. If people have dreams it means that one of their connections is not broken, since memory, observation and sensation is nothing more than one center observing another.[9]

True sleep is the complete disengagement of the centers, one from another:

> A man's sleep does nothing else than interrupt connections between centers. A man's centers never sleep. Since associations are their life, their movement, they never cease, they never stop. A stoppage of associations means death. The movement of associations never stops for an instant in any center, they flow on even in the deepest sleep.[10]

The skillful give the body rest during the day. Doing so represents a real possibility for concentrating work energy: "It is necessary to learn at all costs not to be tense when tension is not needed. When you sit doing nothing, let the body sleep. When you sleep, sleep in such a way that the whole of you sleeps."[11] /In ordinary waking state, if one is asked whether one is conscious of oneself, he or she will assuredly say yes—and in fact for that moment one may be—but the next moment he or she will lapse into the fragmentary, inconsistent, and clouded attention that characterizes this state.

Ordinary waking state is more difficult to appraise, at first, in oneself than in others. Anyone who has a difficult time accepting the notion that as we are, we have but few moments of true self-consciousness, can make a study of the loose jaws and vacant stares of people in public places and in situations where they do not think that they are being observed—the streets of any city or the busses or department stores. Extrapolating from the realization that others walk, talk, eat, work, marry, divorce, and in general spend their lives in a state of almost complete inattention, to the application of this knowledge to one's own life and the acceptance of this truth about oneself may be painful and daring, but it requires only a minimally small deductive leap.

Above sleep states and ordinary waking state there are states of consciousness that may occur as flashes or peak experiences. Those who have devoted themselves to inner work agree that although such states are more likely to occur during or after intense inner effort, effortful striving is utterly insufficient to attract them. Krishnamurti, curried from an early age to be the Messiah of the Theosophists with a life of total meditative discipline, describes many such experiences in his published journals of the years long after he eschewed religious practice and belief as childish. He muses:

> Why should all this happen to us? No explanation is good enough, though one can invent a dozen. But certain things are fairly clear. 1. One must be wholly "indifferent" to its coming and going. 2. There must be no desire to continue the experience or to store it away in memory. 3. There must be a certain physical sensitivity, a certain indifference to comfort. 4. There must be self-critical humorous approach. But even if one had all these, by chance, not through deliberate cultivation and humility, even then, they are not enough. Something totally different is necessary or nothing is necessary. It must come and you can never go after it, do what you will. You can also add love to the list but it is beyond love. One thing is certain, the brain can never comprehend it nor can it contain it. Blessed is he to whom it is given. And you can add also a still, quiet brain.[12]

As we are now we can know little more of the possible higher states of consciousness than what we can assimilate from the reports collected in such works as William James' *The Varieties of Religious Experience*[13] and Richard Bucke's *Cosmic Consciousness*.[14] Such experiences are as relatively inaccessible to modern people as was Tibet to their Medieval counterparts, though the psychedelic revolution has given us what amounts to filmed travelogs that may have increased our wanderlust. We are like householders who own a beautiful mansion of four levels, each floor more sumptuous than the one below it, but we have forgotten how to get upstairs. We live in privation and darkness in the kitchen and the basement, disputing about whether "livingrooms" exist.

THE PSYCHOPATHOLOGY OF ORDINARY WAKING STATE

What keeps us out of the upper floors of our mansion? Obstacles to higher levels of consciousness are abundant in daily life: they are our legacy from generations past. Perhaps the most central is *identification,* the basic flavor of ordinary waking state. "In this state man has no separate awareness. He is lost in whatever he happens to be doing, feeling, thinking. Because he is lost, immersed, not present to himself, this condition is known . . . as a state of waking sleep."[15]

Identification is the opposite of self-consciousness. In a state of identification one does not remember oneself. One is lost to oneself. Attention is directed outward, and no awarness is left over for inner states. And ordinary life is almost totally spent in states of identification.

Identifying with other people's expectations is called *considering.* We can distinguish two kinds of considering, internal and external. Internal considering is based on the feeling of deficiency that a person in the less developed states feels most of the time—in this case the deficiency is felt when people fail to give us sufficient attention or appreciation. It is keeping internal accounts of what we have given and what is, therefore, owed us, and feeling bad, stepped upon, and hurt when others don't pay up. It cannot occur without identification.

External considering, on the other hand, is the practice of empathy and tact. It is true considerateness. It is dependent, therefore, on a certain reliability and consistency of attention and effort on the part of the one who aspires to practice it. Interestingly, attempts at external considering often turn into internal considering when the person making the effort to consider another in the external sense finds no gratitude or caring given in return. External con-

sidering must be its own reward and can expect nothing to be recip-
rocated.

Lying is another inevitable aspect of ordinary waking state
and is so pervasive that Ouspensky[16] proposed that human psychology could be renamed the psychology of lying. Lying, in Gurdjieff's sense, is speaking about that which we do not know. Lying
is obviously present in the chatter of cocktail parties and the lectures of those who know only partially or theoretically and yet
profess to have real understanding. Since all knowledge is intercon-
nected, the presentation of one aspect of truth usually involves
lying.

Gurdjieff differentiates between knowledge and understanding, and this distinction is relevant to the idea of human lying. Knowledge—the acquisition of facts, data, information—is useful in human development only to the degree that it is absorbed or assimilated by one's being, that is, to the degree to which it is understood.
If something is known but not understood there will be lying about
it, for one cannot convey a truth one does not understand.

The thinking of ordinary people occurs when something "occurs to one." It is mechanical chatter, colored by lying, which is
not under any control. Formatory apparatus, the moving part of
intellectual center, is incapable of comprehending orders of truth
higher than the dualistic: thus the ordinary individual is third-force
blind. He sees things in terms of opposites—cause and effect, good
and evil, truth and falsity, seeing duality but not trinity. Since, as
we have seen, the laws of nature are trialectic rather than dialectic,
lying and all other mechanical thought must be considered serious
impediments to self-development.

Another related characteristic of ordinary waking state that
is a useless energy leak and an obstacle to the development of
higher states of consciousness is unnecessary talking. We spend our
lives talking, either outwardly or inwardly. Idle talk is mechanical,
involves imagination and lying, and encourages identification. This
is a key issue, a central theme in many sacred technologies. Don
Juan, for example, explains that the development of a warrior rests
upon "stopping the internal dialogue."[17] Unnecessary talking is related to other unnecessary physical movements and bodily ten-
sions, twitches, fidgeting, finger drumming, foot tapping, grimacing,
and so on, which serve to drain the daily ration of energy that
might, if one but knew how, be used for increasing the level of
available attention.

This brings us to the idea of imagination, the body of unreal-
istic notions about themselves that ordinary people hold as un-

questionable truth. When the word "imagination" is used in the Gurdjieff sense the creative imagination of Leonardo, Rembrandt, Bach or Beethoven or Brahms is not meant. What is meant is something far more commonplace—the delusional system that each of us learns to believe to be the facts of life. This is a form of lying. For example, one is not typically conscious of oneself and yet one believes one is. One is not able to control one's actions and yet one thinks one can. Imagination goes on overtly and covertly all the time. It saps motivation for self-development; for if I do not admit that I am in a state of inattention, what will cause me to wish to change? The urge or impetus to work toward self-consciousness can arise only when the illusion of having capacities we do not actually possess falls away.

Let us consider, finally, the emotional manifestations of ordinary waking state. *Inability to love* is directly related to the inability to be truly considerate, the inability to pay attention, the plurality of "I's" that is the human plight. Although we all need love, we are unable to provide it as we are. "Begin by loving plants and animals, then perhaps you will learn to love people,"[18] says Gurdjieff. In the Gurdjieff literature there are very few references to love, since it is beyond the capacity of ordinary human beings. As we are we can react only to stimuli according to the laws of mechanical association, and according to which "I" is in charge at the moment. In response to a question about the place of love in his teaching, Gurdjieff once said:

> With ordinary love goes hate. I love this. I hate that. Today I love you, next week, or next hour, or next minute, I hate you. He who can really love can *be;* he who can be, can do, he who can do, *is.* To know about real love one must forget all about love and must look for direction. We love because something in ourselves combines with another's emanations from instinctive center, emotional center or intellectual center; or it may be from influences of external form; or from feelings—I love you because you love me, or because you don't love me; suggestions of others; sense of superiority; from pity; and for many other reasons, subjective and egoistic. We allow ourselves to be influenced. Everything attracts or repels. There is the love of sex, which is ordinarily known as "love" between men and women—when this disappears a man and a woman no longer "love" each other. There is the love of feeling, which evokes the opposite and makes people suffer. Later, we will talk about conscious love.[19]

The search for sources of love and objects of love must be disappointing and fruitless, based as it is on the mechanical orientation of sleeping psyches, and the degree to which it is given energy and to which it fascinates the attention is a major obstacle in the development of self-consciousness.

The feelings of ordinary people are made up almost entirely of *negative emotions,* although they are often rather successfully hidden by a polite mask. These negative emotions are triggered by identification and internal considering. Much of what motivates human activity is negative emotion, as anyone who picks up a newspaper can see. Mankind has an enormous repertoire of negativities: there are the basic passions of anger, envy, pride, vanity, hate, sloth, fear; the negative moods such as self-pity, depression, resentment, despair, boredom, irritability; the forms of sentimentality, including much of what is called humanitarianism and love; the forms of negative intellectual bias such as cynicism, argumentativeness, pessimism, suspicion. The list could go on and on. And what seems to be positive in the emotional states experienced by people in ordinary waking state can go sour and turn into negativity with just a little pressure on one of what Gurdjieff called our "corns"—sensitive psychological issues and images which are generally founded on pride or vanity.

THE SYSTEMATIC DISTORTION OF EXPERIENCE OF ORDINARY WAKING STATE

According to Gurdjieff, the ordinary human being experiences the world in such a way that he or she is generally content with his situation, attains a certain amount of pleasure and enjoyment, and finds life tolerable without progress toward self-realization. This feeling of contentment keeps us from striving for higher levels of consciousness and thus ensures that we will continue to serve nature's immediate purpose of transmitting energy from the upper realms of the ray of creation to its growing tip, the moon. The delusion of contentment arises from the effects of "a special organ with a property such that, first, they should perceive reality topsyturvy and secondly, that every repeated impression from outside should crystallize in them data which would engender factors for evoking in them pleasure and enjoyment . . ."[20] This "organ" he calls *Kundabuffer.* Kundabuffer has been removed, it is said, but its effect lingers on. Its residue produces a kind of "opiate of the people" that makes us forget about the terrors of mortality, of utter helplessness and helps us rationalize and lie to ourselves about our state, and to so misperceive the world that we shudder when a mouse runs across the room and feel no fear—in fact, cannot even imagine—the prospect of our own death.

The effects of Kundabuffer are such a serious impediment to

self-realization that Beelzebub remarks, in the concluding statements of *All and Everything:*

> The sole means now for saving beings of the planet Earth would be to implant again into their essences a new organ, an organ like Kundabuffer, but this time of such properties that every one of these unfortunates during the process of existence should constantly sense and be cognizant of the inevitability of his death as well as of the death of everyone upon whom his eyes or attention rests.[21]

ESSENCE AND PERSONALITY

Every human being is, according to Gurdjieff, born with an essential nature. This "essence" is not a *tabula rasa,* a blank or amorphous mass, although it has blank areas in which the influences of life experience make their imprints. It is a real individual identity with its own tendencies and predispositions, already colored by the configuration of stars and planets at the moment of its birth, and it will grow, if not stifled, into self-conscious adulthood. In this process virtually every one of us, like the king's son, Prince Dhat, in the ancient Sufi allegory, falls into the stupor that is ordinary waking state and forgets his origin and destiny.[22]

A little child acts in ways that reflect the truth about his being. He or she is not manipulative; he or she acts in good faith, as it were. But as socialization begins, personality begins to form. The child learns to modify his or her behavior to fit in with culturally approved patterns of conduct. This learning occurs partly through intentional training and partly through a natural tendency to imitate. As an inevitable consequence of the lengthy period of human social dependence (and the lack of instinctive constraints that are present in lower animals) we thus acquire sets of habits, roles, tastes, preferences, concepts, preconceptions and prejudices, desires and felt needs, all of which reflect family and cultural milieu and not necessarily innate tendencies and predispositions. These make up personality. An anonymous author describes this situation poignantly:

> How is it possible to lose a self? The treachery, unknown and unthinkable, begins with our secret psychic death in childhood . . . it is a perfect double crime in which he him-it is not just this simple murder of a psyche [sic] . . . the tiny self gradually and unwittingly takes part. He has not been accepted for himself, *as he is.* Oh, they "love" him, but they want him or force him or expect him to be different! Therefore *he must be unacceptable.* He himself learns to believe it and at last even takes it for granted. He

has truly given himself up. No matter now whether he obeys them, whether he clings, rebels or withdraws—his behavior, his perform- ance is all that matters. His center of gravity is in "them," not in himself—yet if he so much as noticed it he'd think it natural enough. And the whole thing is entirely plausible; all invisible, automatic and anonymous!

This is the perfect paradox. Everything looks normal; no crime was intended; there is no corpse, no guilt. All we can see is the sun rising and setting as usual. But what has happened? He has been rejected not only by them, but by himself. (He is actually without a self.) What has he lost? Just the one true and vital part of himself: his own yes-feeling, which is his very capacity for growth, his root system. But alas, he is not dead. "Life" goes on, and so must he. From the moment he gives himself up, and to the extent that he does so, all unknowingly he sets about to create and maintain a pseudoself. But this is an expediency—a self with- out wishes. This one shall be loved (or feared) where he is de- spised, strong where he is weak; it shall go through the motions (oh, but they are caricatures!) not for fun or joy but for survival; not simply because it wants to move but because it has to obey. This necessity is not life—not his life—it is a defense mechanism against death. It is also the machine of death. From now on he will be torn apart by compulsive (unconscious) conflicts into paralysis, every moment and every instant cancelling out his being, his integ- rity; and all the while he is disguised as a normal person and ex- pected to behave like one!

In a word, I saw that we *become* neurotic seeking or defending a pseudo-self, a self-system; and we *are* neurotic to the extent that we are self-less.[23]

In the best of all possible worlds the acquired habits of per- sonality would be available to one's essential nature and would help one to function adequately in the social context in which he or she lived, and for a realized being this undoubtedly is the case. The or- dinary person, unfortunately, lacks the ability to make use of per- sonality to carry out essential wishes. What is essential can mani- fest only in the simplest instinctive behavior and in primitive emo- tions. The rest of behavior is controlled, as we have seen, by an accidental progression of "I's" that comprise his or her personality. And personality may or may not resemble essence.

People who lead simple lives close to nature may develop in such a way that personality is a minor part or passive element in their psychological makeup, but they are the rare exceptions in a world in which each adult relies almost totally on personality in whatever he or she does for a living, in public behavior, in intimate relationships, in virtually all aspects of daily existence. In most of us personality is active and essence passive: personality determines our values and beliefs, profession, religious convictions, and philosophy of living. Personality, not essence, is responsible for the vast quantities of books and articles that fill the libraries of the world, for few indeed speak from or to essence; personality creates most visual art; it speaks in the highest sentiments of statesmen. Personality even projects a God and prays to that projection.

Essence is what is one's own. Personality is what is not one's own, what may be changed by changing conditions or artificially removed with hypnosis, drugs, or special exercises. Gurdjieff demonstrated this to his early pupils dramatically by temporarily stripping two individuals of their personalities for purposes of comparison.[24] Those who have had some acquaintance with psychedelic drugs may have experienced essence in themselves or observed it in others, for some psychotropic substances may have the effect of anesthetizing personality briefly so that essence can appear without distortion.

ESSENCE AND PERSONALITY COMPARED

Essence	Personality
Innate	Acquired
What is a person's own	What is "not one's own"
The truth in a human being	The false in a human being
Develops into one's individuality	Provides the information necessary to work on self
Controlled by fate	Controlled by accident

All this is not to say that essence is always noble and beautiful while personality is an alien crust of useless cultural barnacles. According to Gurdjieff, "as a rule a man's essence is either primitive, savage and childish, or else simply stupid."[25] The essences of many are actually dead, though they continue to live seemingly normal lives. The development of essence to maturity, when it will embody everything that is true and real in a person's being, depends on work on oneself, and work on oneself depends on a balance between a relatively healthy essence and a personality that is not crushingly heavy—as it is in the case of the "rich man" who cannot get into heaven. Both are necessary for self-development, for without the acquisition of personality there will be no wish to attain higher states of consciousness, no dissatisfaction with everyday existance; and without essence there will be no basis of development.

*Man's higher nature rests upon man's lower nature,
needing it as a foundation and collapsing without
this foundation.*

—Abraham Maslow

*Each Perfected Man is in a sense the same as each
other one. This means that, correctly attuned
through the energy of the School, a disciple can
come into communication with all the Great Ones,
just as they are in communication with each other,
across time and place . . .
The duties and practices of the School form
one whole: the Truth, the manner of teaching and
the participants form* one hand, *in which the ignor-
ant may see only the dissimilarity of the fingers,
not the combined action of the hand itself.*

—Bahaudin Naqshband

CHAPTER FOUR

Human Possibilities

Although the picture of the ordinary human state as presented by Gurdjieff might be thought of as quite grim, it is not at all without hope. The qualities one attributes to oneself through imagination and lying can actually be attained: there can be a real and unchanging "I," there can be action that is not reaction—the virtues and the understanding of the great perfection are not entirely beyond our reach.

Every human being is born with the same right to develop, yet there are noticeable degrees of potential for inner growth. Man Number One is somewhat less permeable to the kinds of influences that attract people to inner work than is Man Number Two, and Man Number Two, in turn, is not as likely to heed these messages as is Man Number Three. Looking at the possibilities for spiritual attainment from the point of view of attitude, it is important that an ordinary person be a "good householder" rather than a "tramp" or a "lunatic" if he or she is to begin to realize the full human potential. A good householder is a person who is capable, well oriented in life, able to do his or her duty—and who no longer believes fully in life's goals and aims as defined by the culture. A tramp is someone who believes in very little at all, who cannot or does not wish to live up to any responsibility. Tramps are more open minded than lunatics who think they can do, think they know, believe in unrealities. Lunatics are full of their own false understanding and imagined knowledge and are too fascinated with their own phantasmagoria to see anything else, a state of being that prompted one Zen master to respond by pouring more and more tea into his visitor's cup until its message was soaked in: our cup must be emptied for the dharma to be received. Each of us has a tramp and a lunatic within, so to speak, which provide resistance to personal development through their antagonistic or complacent attitudes. In speaking of the Russian peasant or *obyvatel* as typifying the good house-

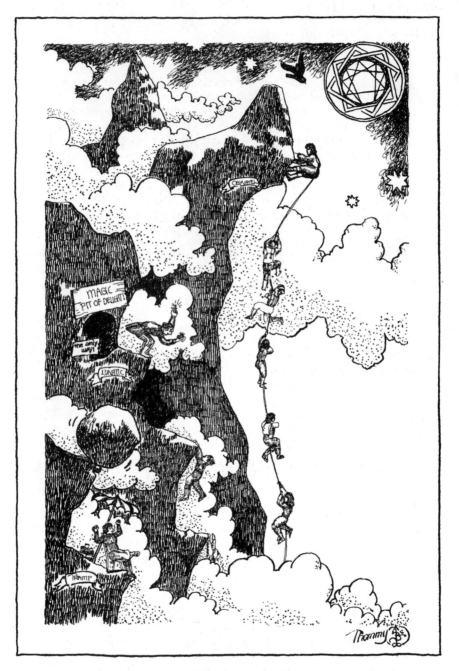

Every human being is born with the same right and ability to develop—
but some are more likely to do it than others.

holder attitude, Gurdjieff explained:

> People who are definitely thinking about ways, particularly people of intellectual ways, very often look down on the *obyvatel* and in general despise the virtues of the *obyvatel*. But they only show by this their own personal unsuitability for any way whatever. Because no way can begin from a level lower than the *obyvatel*. This is very often lost sight of on people who are unable to organize their own personal lives, who are too weak to struggle with and conquer life, dream of the ways, or what they consider are ways, because they think it will be easier for them than life and because this, so to speak, justifies their weakness and their inadaptability. A man who can be a good *obyvatel* is much more helpful from the point of view of the way than a "tramp" who thinks himself much higher than an *obyvatel*. I call "tramps" all the so-called intelligentsia—artists, poets, any kind of "bohemian" in general, who despises the *obyvatel* and who at the same time would be unable to exist without him. Ability to orientate oneself is a very useful quality from the point of view of work. A good *obyvatel* should be able to support at least twenty persons by his own labor. What is a man worth who is unable to do this?[1]

In addition to being able to do the ordinary as a foundation upon which the extraordinary can come into being, one must find within oneself an attraction toward self-development. Gurdjieff calls this *magnetic center*. Each person grows up surrounded by influences coming from within life and other influences coming from sources of conscious origin, outside of ordinary life. These influences from above (or from an inner circle of humanity) begin to collect within an individual and eventually, if there are enough of them, they develop sufficient mass, so to speak, to affect orientation, to produce a feeling of need for self-development or at least a vague discontent. The values and goals of everyday life then become a context for a search, a hankering after a certain kind of reading, a growing inclination to be with people who are also concerned with such things. Ouspensky quotes Gurdjieff's description of the effect of magnetic center on personal orientation:

> If the magnetic center receives sufficient nourishment and if there is no strong resistance on the part of the other sides of a man's personality which are the result of influences created in life, the magnetic center begins to influence a man's orientation, obliging him to turn round and even to move in a certain direction. When the magnetic center attains sufficient force and development, a man already understands the idea of a way and he begins to look for the way. The search for the way may take many years and may lead to nothing. This depends upon conditions,

upon circumstances, upon the power of the magnetic center, upon the power and the direction of inner tendencies which are not concerned with this search and which may divert a man at the very moment when the possibility of finding the way appears.[2]

If he or she is lucky, a person who has begun to seek may come upon another person, one who has genuine knowledge about how to develop. Then he or she comes under the sway of a third kind of influence: that which can be transmitted only personally from master to pupil. Then begins a course of instruction that may lead to inner harmony and unity, altered states, and to higher and higher levels of being.

THE FOUR WAYS

In orienting oneself toward the good, the beautiful and the true and aligning oneself with what is emanating from sources more conscious than ordinary, there are three traditional religious approaches. These paths or ways correspond to the three types of ordinary human beings, Man Number One, Man Number Two and Man Number Three, in the relative importance or stress given to the three functions. These traditional ways are:

1.   The way of the fakir;

2.   The way of the monk;

3.   The way of the yogi.

The fakir develops mastery of the lowest story, the physical body, by enduring tortuous physical postures or exercises. Some fakirs assume a painful position such as standing on one leg or balancing on fingers and toes, and they maintain it for years. In so doing they strengthen will. The way of the fakir requires very little knowledge. Disciples simply stay in the general vicinity of one who has attained and learn by imitation. If a fakir does actually achieve an unbendable will he must still develop the other two basic functions and sometimes, in the rare event that he is found and taken on by a skilled master, this may be possible.

The way of the monk is the way of devotion, religious sacrifice and faith. The emotional center is the focus of work in this way, which appeals to Man Number Two. Emotions are transcended and self-mastery attained when all petty desires are subjugated to the love of God. But even if this state of being is attained, the monk can only be a "silly saint" if he or she does not go on to develop the physical and intellectual functions correspondingly.

The way of the yogi is the path of knowledge, the path which Man Number Three finds most congenial. Again, though the yogi

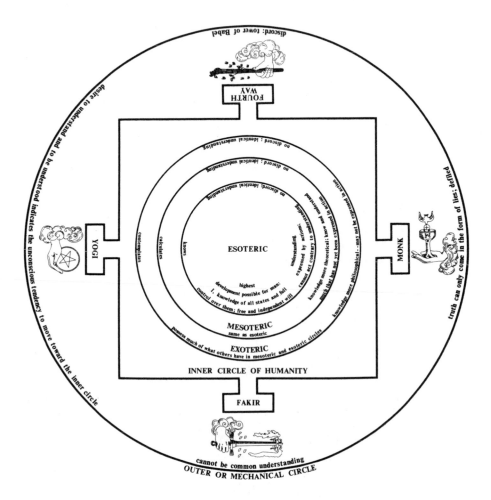

FOUR GATES OR WAYS
(three tied to permanent religious forms; fourth
appears and disappears for definite undertakings)

achieves total understanding it will be impotent and dry without the other functions at the same level. New efforts and new studies will have to follow if unity is to be attained.

The fakir, the monk and the yogi must renounce the world, abstain from family life and devote their full energies to personal development. At the beginning of each of these ways, at the initiation of work, one must turn one's back upon the world and die to the past.

There is another way, the fourth way, for those who want to remain "in the world but not of it." Unlike the traditional religious ways, the fourth way has no permanent institutions. It appears and disappears according to the time, the place and the people. In following this approach to self-realization the seeker renounces renunciation. Work is done on all three stories of the "food factory" at once and thus when and if the end result is attained, it is already attained in all three functions simultaneously. Because it makes use of one's own life situation without requiring outward changes it is a possible path for all types of people. The Gurdjieff work is in the tradition of fourth way schools.

The names of the four ways need not be misleading to students of world religion if it is remembered that whether a particular sect or tradition belongs to one or another of the ways depends not on whether its adherents call themselves monks or yogis but on the relative predominance of centers. A Zen monk meditating on a koan is, though called a monk, following the way of the yogi as defined here; those practicing bhakti yoga, chanting in rapture at the feet of the guru, are on the way of the monk.

Each of the four ways may lead the aspirant from the samsaric complexities and sufferings of ordinary waking state—the daily bread of the masses of people who make up what might be called the outer circle of humanity—into the realm of perfected beings, the inner circle of those who have attained. Though each of the four ways must by the very nature of the ordinary world give the teachings in defiled form (for that is all that can be heard in the world of lies and confusion) there is perfect agreement among those who have attained, whatever their path may have been. Entry into the inner circle means further growth in communion with like beings and an end to uncertainty and discord.

HIGHER STATES OF CONSCIOUSNESS

In addition to the sleep and waking sleep that alternate in the lives of almost everyone there are other possible ways of being, states in which perception is clear and undistorted, emotion spa-

In addition to the sleep and waking sleep that alternate in the lives of almost everyone, there are other possible states of consciousness.

cious and uncontracted and action beyond the pleasure principle. These states are natural to human beings and have been forfeited in favor of psychological complexities—basically, as we have seen, through a clouding of consciousness acquired by cultural infection in early childhood. Gurdjieff differentiates two levels of conscious functioning above the ordinary: self-consciousness and objective consciousness.

Self-consciousness occurs spontaneously for brief moments that often leave particularly vivid memories behind them. These are the high moments that may occur in situations of great danger, intense emotion, or extraordinary stress. Then attention is clear, impartial and relatively complete and is divided between self and environment so that action unfolds spontaneously, appropriately and sometimes even heroically. Self-consciousness can also become a way of being. There are many levels of its development. It starts with a division into two, as some of the attention is given to oneself and some is available to perceive the environment. In its fullest form, the basic contraction of ego is absent, producing a particular quality of experience described by Mme. Ouspensky like this:

> What is the first characteristic of self-remembering? In this state man is not center. He is not separate. Sitting in a room, he is aware of the whole room, of himself as only one of the objects in it. He is likewise aware of others and does not put himself above them or criticize or judge. This is not love, but it is the beginning of love. In this state a man has no self as he is usually aware of it. It is quite impossible for him to consider or become negative, for the moment he does so the state will vanish.[3]

Above self-consciousness there is a higher state, objective consciousness, which also occurs in spontaneous flashes. Such moments are life's "peak experiences"—or they are totally forgotten as lower centers fall into unconsciousness to protect the body's delicate machinery from unbearably high energy. During states of objective consciousness higher centers are connected to the ordinary ones. One is fully attuned to, and aware of, cosmic laws. Cognition has "limpid clearness and consummate perspicacity," as Long-chen-pa puts it.[4] One understands. One knows. Along with the *knowing* comes an ecstatic or blissful quality of joyful acceptance. This condition, too, may become an ever-present station.

Most of us have tasted this state, but for some it may have been followed by unconsciousness and amnesia as lower centers temporarily blacked out. Because this state is the rarest and most valuable of human experiences, we will give it considerable attention here. An account given by one of Gurdjieff's pupils of an ex-

STATES OF CONSCIOUSNESS

Objective Consciousness	The "enlightened" state . . . Things seem *as they are* . . . Result of inner growth and long work on self . . . Can occur in flashes in all people
Self-Consciousness	The only way to the development of a sustained consciousness . . . Can be acquired by ordinary human beings, also, individuality, will, ability to do . . . Occurs in flashes to ordinary people without work
Ordinary Waking State "Sleep"	Almost entirely subjective . . . Can be active—but everything *happens* . . . Characterized by identification, lying, mechanicality, considering, emotional deficiency . . . More dangerous than ordinary sleep
Ordinary Sleep	Entirely subjective . . . Connections between centers partially broken . . . Characterized by passivity, immersion in dreams

perience that took place while he was spending the summer in the Gurdjieff-inspired architectural community, Taliesin, will serve as an introduction:

> It was during this summer that I had the first deep and vivid experience of higher consciousness. The three previous experiences of this unexpected impact of higher forces were a taste of real consciousness of self. The present one was different. One hot day I was walking from the house across the fields to bathe in the Wisconsin River. About half way a strange and wonderful force began to enter into me and permeate my whole being, and filled me with light and power. I stopped and stood still and let the force flow. Although I was aware of my surroundings—the forest and fields and the hot sun, they were only a background to the inner experience; all anxieties and cares of ordinary life dropped away; at the same time I saw myself and my relations with people quite clearly; I saw the pattern of my life, my organism moving as it were along its appointed path. There was time no longer, and an understanding of the whole of life seemed possible for me. It was as if for a few moments I had entered into my real life; and the outer life, which had seemed so important and took up all my time, was not the real life but something ephemeral, a sort of cinema film with which I was identified. Only the inner something was eternal—I, the real self of me. I AM.[5]

The possibility of objective consciousness exists for those following any of the four ways. There is a feeling of interpenetration of all things—St. John of the Cross speaks of being "wounded by Christ"—and a sense of participation in a reality that transcends time and space and yet seems to be within. When Rabia, the great woman saint of Islam was asked to come and delight in the beauty of the creation, she replied that she was looking inward to delight in the Creator. Here is an account of an inward journey of Sri Aurobindo's associate, the Mother:

> ... To find the soul one must step back from the surface, withdraw deep within, and enter, enter, go down, far down into a very deep hole, silent, still; and then down there, is something warm, tranquil, rich in contents and very still, and very full, like a sweetness —this is the soul. And if one persists and is conscious in oneself, a sort of plenitude comes which gives the impression of something complete holding unfathomable profundities. And one feels that if one entered there many secrets would be revealed, like the reflection in calm, peaceful waters of something which is eternal. And the limits of time are no more. One has the impression of having always been and of being for eternity.[6]

And this from the days just before Krishnamurti's transformation:

> There was a man mending the road; that man was myself; the pickaxe he held was myself; the very stone which he was breaking up was part of me; the tender blade of grass was my very being; and the tree beside the man was myself. I could almost think and feel like the roadmender, and I could feel the wind passing through the tree, and the little ant on the blade of grass I could feel. The birds, the dust, and the very noise were part of me. Just then there was a car passing by at some distance; I was the driver, the engine, and the tyres; as the car went further away from me, I was going away from myself. I was in everything, or rather everything was in me, inanimate and animate, the mountain, the worm, and all breathing things. All day long I remained in this happy condition.[7]

The experience is often described as having to do with light, illumination, enlightenment. Here is an account in a different cultural context, by the contemporary Indian saint, Swami Muktananda Paramhansa:

> Now I was meditating as before. Lord Nityananda suddenly administered an inner jolt. Immediately, the rays of the red aura gleamed in my 72,000 nerves and innumerable blood particles. The white flame appeared along with its support, the black light; and then the dear, the beloved Blue Pearl, the ground of all! Immediately my meditation became more intense. My vision focussed

upwards. While I was gazing at the tiny Blue Pearl, it began to expand in all directions, spreading its blue radiance. The entire region from earth to sky became irradiated. It was Pearl no longer, having enlarged into the shining, sparkling infinite Light. This has been designated by the scriptural authors or the seers of the highest truth as the conscious light of Chiti. I actually saw the universe arise from this expanding light like clouds of smoke from a fire. The cosmos appeared in the conscious light and the conscious light in the cosmos like threads in a cloth and cloth in threads. Just as one seed grows into a tree, shooting forth twigs, leaves, blossoms and fruit, similarly the selfsame Chiti becomes, in Her own being, birds and animals, germs and insects, angels and demons, men and women. I perceived the refulgent, divinely beautiful conscious light calmly throbbing as supreme bliss on all sides, within and without, above and below. Though my eyes were open, I was in meditation. Just as a diver descending into water, surrounded by water and water alone on all sides, so also was I completely enveloped by that conscious light. In this state, the universe vanished and I beheld only pure effulgence surging all around . . .[8]

As a final example, here is a vivid experience reported by a solitary Buddhist practicing in New Zealand, making use of information he had gleaned from books:

. . . I took the kung an "All things are returnable to the One, to where does the One return?" and held it diligently. At first the mind was crowded with thoughts but gradually a change took place until I was able to clear my mind of all but the kung an. Then I could go no further. All seemed lost. I felt useless and lost. But I was determined and withdrew to solitude in the mountains where I walked and worked until bodily exhausted, all the while keeping the kung an in my mind.

Then one day I stopped by a river and sat exhausted. Suddenly I heard, not with my ears it seemed, the sigh of the wind in the trees. Immediately I passed from my state of exhaustion into one where I was so relaxed I felt open to total flow, over and round and through my body. Everything was dripping with white-hot light or electricity (although there were no objects as such) and it was as though I was watching the whole cosmos coming into being, constantly, molten. How can there be so much light? Layers and layers of light upon light. All is illumination. The dominant impression was that of entering into the very marrow of existence— no forms, no personalities, no deities, just bliss.[9]

States similar to objective consciousness are also reported by those who experiment with mind-altering drugs. According to Gurdjieff, drugs may be useful to give a taste of what these states are like, but objective consciousness can be approached legitimately only through the careful development of sustained self-consciousness. Only then can this state become an abiding and invulnerable way of being.

THE STAGES OF HUMAN DEVELOPMENT

In addition to the three human types we have already classified according to the predominance of thinking, feeling or moving-instinctive functioning, there are higher possibilities for human development. Man Number One, Two or Three is born but the higher levels of human beings—that is, Men Number Four, Five, Six and Seven, are always the results of efforts made on one of the ways that have come to fruition.

THE SEVEN LEVELS OF HUMAN DEVELOPMENT

7   Will; consciousness; permanent and unchanging "I"; individuality; immortality.

6   Same qualities as level 7 although some are not completely permanent. Complete knowledge—but it still can be lost.

5   Has unity; already crystallized. Cannot go back accidentally to previous levels of development. Whole and indivisible knowledge; what is known is known with the whole being.

4   Permanent center of gravity in the ideas, valuation and relation to inner work. Centers becoming balanced. Beginning to actually observe self and know aim. Already receiving knowledge from higher levels and beginning to get free from subjective elements.
       Cannot be born nor develop accidentally as the result of ordinary influences.

3   2   1

Center of gravity in intellectual center; everything from theories, mental constructions. Wants proofs and systems.

Center of gravity in emotional center. Knowledge of likes and dislikes, of preferences and aversions. Wants something pleasant, or if sick, something loathsome.

Center of gravity in moving-instinctive center; knowledge by imitation and instinct. Wants gratification of lusts and comfort.

No matter what one's native predisposition, with work and good fortune the first quantic leap is to the state called Man Number Four. Man Number Four has a permanent center of gravity which consists of the determination to develop, an aim around which the rest of one's life now revolves. This is the beginning of real evolution. The centers are beginning to become balanced and harmonious in operation. There is beginning to be real knowledge about oneself and an understanding of where one is going.

Man Number Five has reached inner unity through the crystalization of a permanent "I." There is no longer any falling back except by intentionally undergoing an agonizing decrystallization in the rare event that crystallization has taken place on the wrong foundation because the individual has not first been Man Number Four. Such wrong crystallization produces "hasnamuss" individuals whose real ability to "do" is inevitably distorted by an insufficiently tamed personal ego, causing suffering to others. If the crystallization occurs correctly, however, an individual at this level of development is immeasurably different from ordinary people in the ability to know deeply and clearly and to act in the light of real understanding.

The highest levels of attainment represent all we can hope to be. Man Number Six has all the attributes of Man Number Seven except that some of them are not permanent. Man Number Seven possesses all the qualities a human being can have: will, full consciousness, a permanent and unchanging "I," individuality and immortality.

EVOLUTION, DEATH AND IMMORTALITY

Immortality is possible for a human being only to the degree to which he or she has developed embodiments of himself or herself beyond the ordinary physical body. Many esoteric traditions describe spiritual development in terms of four bodies, each more subtle and finer than the last, which stand in definite relation to one another.

In Gurdjieff's teachings the first body is the familiar physical body that each human being identifies as himself or herself. This is the *carnal body* in Christian terminology. It is all one has without work on oneself and when death occurs it returns to dust.

Under certain conditions a second body, called the *astral body* or body kesdjan by Gurdjieff, sometimes grows within the physical body. This new body is not at all necessary for a person to have, and in fact it is possible to appear to be very highly developed intellectually and emotionally—and even spiritually—without one. Body kesdjan is something of a luxury. The physical body has all the functions of the astral body or analogs of them, and, indeed, of all the higher bodies. It can work with the same energies and process approximately the same substances. The difference is that while the physical body can use these energies and substances, they pass through it and are not, so to speak, owned. The functions of the physical body govern the processing and they, in turn, are under the control of general laws. Will does not exist. Reaction is all that is possible for a person with only a physical body though the repertoire of reactions may seem to be as subtle and attuned as the actions of a more highly evolved person to those without experience in personal evolution.

The third body is related to intellectual functioning, to the opening of the higher thinking faculty. It is called the spiritual or *mental body*. The fourth is the causal or *divine body* and is related to the functioning of all centers in unified harmony and with intention. Only Man Number Seven, who has developed all four bodies, can be called, in Gurdjieff's phrase, "man without quotation marks."

Gurdjieff compares the human being with his or her thoughts, feelings and physiology to a coachman driving a horse-drawn hackney carriage. The carriage is analogous to the physical body, the horse is the emotions, the coachman, dressed in a shabby cloak, a brand new top hat which is "an exact replica of Rockefeller's" and

THE FOUR BODIES AND THE RAY OF CREATION

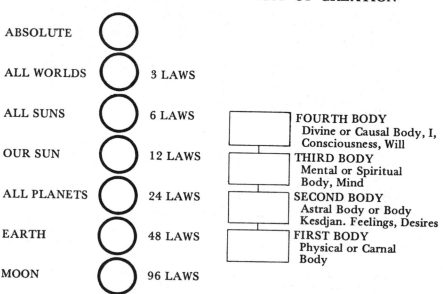

ABSOLUTE

ALL WORLDS — 3 LAWS

ALL SUNS — 6 LAWS

FOURTH BODY
Divine or Causal Body, I, Consciousness, Will

OUR SUN — 12 LAWS

THIRD BODY
Mental or Spiritual Body, Mind

ALL PLANETS — 24 LAWS

SECOND BODY
Astral Body or Body Kesdjan. Feelings, Desires

EARTH — 48 LAWS

FIRST BODY
Physical or Carnal Body

MOON — 96 LAWS

Gurdjieff compares the human being to a coachman driving a horse-drawn hackney carriage. Who is the master?

in his buttonhole sporting a giant chrysanthemum, represents the thinking apparatus. There is also a passenger in the box who has hired the cab—this is whatever "I" is there at the moment. Though the carriage may be of the latest style it is at the mercy of the coachman, who has never understood it and thus never cleans it properly. And although the carriage was originally designed to lubricate itself in motion, as the bumps and shocks of byways spread the oil around its moving parts, today's smooth highways render that kind of greasing unlikely. The horse, says Gurdjieff, has hardly any understanding of the coachman's words and signals and, worse,

> . . . has never received any special education, but has been molded exclusively under the influence of constant thrashings and vile abuse. It has always been kept tied up; and for food, instead of oats and hay, there is given to it merely straw which is utterly worthless for its real needs. Never having seen in any of the manifestations towards it even the least love or friendliness, the horse is now ready to surrender itself completely to anybody who gives it the slightest caress.[10]

The coachman-cabby sits sleepily in the box, ready to go anywhere for anyone who offers him a fare (as long as it doesn't cause him too much trouble) and anywhere at all for a fare plus tip.

Looking at this analogy from the point of view of what a human being might become, the carriage corresponds to the physical body, the horse to the astral body, the coachman to the mental body and the passenger to the divine body or master who, unlike any passerby who might rent the carriage, actually owns, maintains and directs the carriage. The ordinary individual is like an automaton whose actions, desires and thoughts are the products of environmental stimuli and who is, therefore, plagued by the inner conflict of contradictory "wills." The direction of control goes from the outer world to the inner. The development of all the higher bodies reversed the direction of control: the permanent "I" or master is obeyed by the mind and emotions and the body obeys the thoughts and feelings in its turn.

Seen in terms of the ray of creation, the first body is created with the materials of this planet and is therefore destined to return to earth. The second body is made of a finer quality material, that of level 24, and can last after the death of the physical body but is not, strictly speaking, immortal. It will be survived by the third body if there is one. The fourth body is immortal within the limits of the solar system since it is composed of materials that do not belong to the solar system, but to the level beyond it. Thus one person may be immortal and another destined to complete disintegration at the time of death. It all depends upon the level of inner development.

The possibility of levels of relative immortality which are based upon inner work evokes the idea of reincarnation or recurrence, which states, in many versions (depending on the theological or cosmological context in which they are embedded) that something in each human being must retun again and again to life after life until psychological tendencies and biases are totally neutralized. On this topic Gurdjieff was often abrupt and unwilling to teach, since it has the flavor of intellectual fitting games rather than practical import. Ouspensky once plied him for a statement on the subject.

> "This idea of repetition," said G., "is not the full and absolute truth but it is the nearest possible approximation of the truth. In this case truth cannot be expressed in words. But what you say is very near to it. And if you understand why I do not speak of this, you will be still nearer to it. What is the use of a man knowing about recurrence if he is not conscious of it and if he himself does not change? One can say even that if a man does not change, repetition does not exist for him. If you tell him about repetition it will only increase his sleep. Why should he make any efforts today when there is so much time and so many possibilities ahead —the whole of eternity? This is exactly why the system does not say anything about repetition and takes only this one life which we know. The system has neither meaning nor sense without striving for self-change. And work on self-change must begin today, immediately. All laws can be seen in one life. Knowledge about the repetition of lives will add nothing for a man if he does not see how everything repeats itself in one life, that is, in this life, and if he does not strive to change himself in order to escape this repetition. But if he changes something essential in himself, that is, if he attains something, this cannot be lost."[11]

This kind of inner change is the goal of every real religious teaching and practice, for it may give one the capacity to live virtuously, harmoniously, and forever. The human being of the highest attainment assimilates the food, air, and impressions he or she receives as daily bread to the fullest extent possible, for he or she is wise in the ways of delivering the two conscious shocks necessary to bring inner metabolism to completion. This is the aim of the system of study and practice that was transmitted by Gurdjieff to his pupils, and which is now known as the "Gurdjieff work."

The Sufis feel that maturity cannot be achieved alone. They feel there is a need for guidance and discipline. The path is unknown, the night is dark and the road is full of danger. Dangers include preoccupation with selfishness, false visions, misinterpretations of mystical states, arrest in development, fixation in a particular state, appeal to various drugs to create false mystical experiences and not infrequently overwhelming anxiety and insanity.

—Mohammed Shafii

The true way goes over a rope which is not stretched at any great height but just above the ground. It seems more designed to make people stumble than to be walked upon.

—Franz Kafka

CHAPTER FIVE:
The Gurdjieff Work

A man who sleeps cannot "do." With him everything is done in sleep. Sleep is understood here not in the literal sense of our organic sleep, but in the sense of associative existence. First of all he must awake. Having awakened, he will see that as he is he cannot "do." He will have to die voluntarily. When he is dead he may be born. But the being who has just been born must grow and learn. When he has grown and knows, then he will "do."[1]

The method of self-development taught by Gurdjieff is an attempt to liberate individual seekers from the heavy burden of laws under which our place and function in the universe compel us to live. It is the technology of subverting the effects of the organ Kundabuffer, of plugging up energy leaks and tuning the body's machinery for the transformation of various foods, of making personality passive with respect to essence, of increasing knowledge and being, of developing higher bodies, of delivering the first and second conscious shocks.

In order to develop from any of the three ordinary types into higher orders of being it is necessary to crystallize and temper essence into a permanent and unified "I." This is done mainly by instigating a struggle between essence and personality. Both essence and personality are necessary for this work: essence must have personality or it will not wish to develop. Personality provides the material to study, the obstacles to overcome, the temptations to resist, the delusions to invalidate, and in the process of struggling with and testing itself against personality, essence gains in strength and maturity. This battle is what Islam calls the holy war *(jihad)* and in this war the more evenly matched the opposing sides, the greater the intensity of combat and the more thorough the destruction and renewal entailed.

The work, or war, can most profitably take place in the conditions that make up one's daily routine, for the environment, rela-

tionships, habits and responsibilities in which a person finds him
or herself are yet another reflection of the patterns of functioning
acquired in the formation of personality. The organism can be
studied in its native habitat, and patterns of action, feeling and
thought analyzed in terms of the use of energies. Through seeing
the false as the false, the true may of itself come into being.

Because there is no requirement to leave home, family or profession, the Gurdjieff work is perhaps more accessible and easier
to begin than paths of self-realization requiring an initial withdraw-
al from the world. Once fully engaged, however, the process is no
less arduous.

THE BEGINNING

Those who wish to engage in work on themselves according
to the methods of Gurdjieff can expect obstacles to be thrown up
in front of them at the beginning. First there is the problem of
finding a group, which is not as easy as finding the monastery of a
religious order or the ashram of a yogi. People who are practicing
Gurdjieff's techniques are relatively invisible as they go about their
daily round of activities. And they have very little missionary inclination; groups that proselytize are very likely to be imitators.

Gurdjieff emphasized that knowledge cannot belong to all or
even a majority of people, not because anything must be kept secret or retained by an elect few, but because the acquisition of real
knowledge requires great effort on the part of both teacher and
student, master and disciple, and this effort is not often considered
valuable by those who consider themselves seekers. Like everything
else in the cosmos, knowledge is material in nature; and like any
other form of matter it must exist in a limited quantity at any
given place and time. Gurdjieff once made the analogy with gold:

> If we take a certain quantity of gold and decide to gild a cer-
> tain number of objects with it, we must know or calculate, exact-
> ly what number of objects can be gilded with this quantity of
> gold. If we try to gild a greater number, they will be covered with
> gold unevenly, in patches, and will be much worse than if they
> had no gold at all; in fact, we shall lose our gold.
>
> The distribution of knowledge is based on exactly the same
> principle. If knowledge is given to all, nobody will get any. If it is
> preserved among a few, each will receive not only enough to keep,
> but to increase what he receives.
>
> At first glance this theory seems very unjust, since the position
> of those who are, so to speak, denied knowledge in order that
> others may receive a greater share appears to be very sad and un-
> deservedly harder than it ought to be. Actually, however, this is

not so at all; and in the distribution of knowledge there is not the slightest injustice.[2]

Nothing is concealed, no knowledge is withheld, yet Gurdjieff stresses: "He who wants knowledge must himself make the initial efforts to find the source of knowledge and approach it, taking advantage of the help and indications that are given to all, but which people, as a rule, do not want to see or recognize. Knowledge cannot come to people without effort on their own part."[3] Even in the present age when the dharma is available in paperback and when what once was hidden is widely broadcast, the secret protects itself.

Gurdjieff's understanding of the finite nature and materiality of knowledge clearly reflects the influence of the Sarmoun Brotherhood for whom he had sought with such persistence in his youth. Here is a recent account of their activity:

> There are many legends about the Sarmoun-Dargauh ("Court of
> the Bees") and one of them is this. True knowledge, it is asserted,
> exists as a positive commodity, like the honey of a bee. Like honey,
> it can be accumulated. From time to time in human history, how-
> ever, it lies unused and starts to leak away. On those occasions the
> Sarmouni and their associates all over the world collect it and
> store it in a special receptacle. Then, when the time is ripe, they
> release it into the world again, through specially trained emmis-
> saries.[4]

Knowledge is available when the time is ripe, but which of us will take the trouble to do what is necessary to have it? There is a story that undoubtedly has no basis in fact, of how a would-be initiate sought far and wide for the real teachings and at last found the source: a monastery, inaccessible except by a tortuous journey on foot, lost in the remotest of mountains. He made the journey, knocked upon the door, and was refused. Gurdjieff also came to this monastery, looked over the situation, went away, came back with some heavy equipment and graded the road right up to the monastery gates. Then he knocked upon the door and was welcomed.

The question of payment always arises. Some may believe that anything related to spirituality or to self-development should be given away free, but this, to Gurdjieff, is a fundamental mistake. Esoteric knowledge, like anything else in the universe (including our existence) must be paid for—by the effort it takes to find it and assimilate it and even by actual payment in service or money as well. Like Freud, Gurdjieff recognized that people do not value what they do not pay for. Ouspensky put it this way:

Payment is a principle. Payment is necessary not to the school but to the people themselves, for without paying they will not get anything. The idea of payment is very important and it must be understood that payment is absolutely necessary. One can pay in one way or another way and everyone has to find that out for himself. But nobody can *get* anything that he does not pay for. Things cannot be given, they can only be bought. It is magical, not simple. If one has knowledge, one cannot give it to another person, for only if he pays for it can the other person have it. This is a cosmic law.[5]

The notion of the good householder is relevant here. Competence and strength in the world are predictive of strength in the work. The most likely candidates for the fourth way teachings have a trade or profession that they know well and that is valued in the world. Knowing something well, even if it is as simple as making a good cup of coffee, gives one experience in doing a task thoroughly —beginning, middle and end. It also provides financial solidity that frees the attention for inner work.

STAGES ON THE WAY

The Gurdjieff work is very much a group activity. A number of people gathered around a teacher can form a center of gravity for their mutual benefit that one person working independently, however dedicated, cannot have. The group is used to create conditions favorable to work on oneself, to generate energy, to produce psychological heat through interpersonal frictions, to provide mutual support and for many other purposes as well. Becoming part of a group and relating to a teacher is the very first stage of the Gurdjieff work. Reading books and articles and attempting to carry out practices can give a taste of the work but without the group situation and the guidance of another who is at least somewhat more advanced in the work, even the best intentions will gradually but inevitably be diverted from their original orientation by the discontinuities inherent in all processes, as we have seen in the study of the Law of Seven.

After one takes the initial step of finding a group with which to work, the exact order of stages and phases of the process will depend on each individual pattern of unfolding. In working on all three functions (intellectual, emotional, instinctive) simultaneously and allowing, even requiring, life in the world, the Gurdjieff work differs from the three traditional religious paths. It does not focus more on one of the three stories or "brains" than another, though for individuals it is often necessary to concentrate on one

of the centers for a while in order to make up for atrophy that
may have occurred through trauma or disuse in life—as, for example, when a coldly rational person must painfully learn to experience emotions, or an impulsive doer to stop and think. What is
right for one may be useless or even deleterious for another. It is
for this reason, among others, that the actual practices of esoteric
teaching are transmitted orally.

Yet, however individual the actual course of work on oneself
must and will inevitably be, some general directions of work can
be discerned. Three "lines of work" exist in Gurdjieff's teaching:
work for and on oneself; work with and for others; and work in
the service of the ideas of the work, in and for the work itself.
These lines correspond roughly to the three basic functions of
moving-instinctive, emotional and intellectual centers. They may
begin simultaneously or not, but in any case the first line is most
likely to be stressed at first, later more attention is given to the
second line of work, and only the most advanced focus most of
their energies on the third line of work.

THE FIRST LINE OF WORK

The first line of work is an extended attempt to follow the
ancient injunction, "Know thyself." Knowledge about oneself and
the order of things is sought through many channels and at the
same time awareness is enlarged and strengthened to increase the
level of being. Work in this line typically begins with the collection
of information about personal functioning without any attempt to
change. Do I actually know myself, here and now? Know myself
with the kind of objectivity that I can at times apply to others?
Who is this person who goes around under the name of Mr. So-and-
so or Ms. Such-and-such? The only person who can know myself
is myself—no one can do what is required for self-knowledge for
me. And no amount of fantasizing about who or what I am will
substitute for a direct, dispassionate look at the data. C. Daly King,
a student of Orage and leader of early New York groups, gave some
preliminary advice for this sort of self-appraisal. Although the context in which it is given is obviously dated, in light of present government probes, in substance it is still valuable:

> To get the feel of this thing let us have a practice run. Take some-
> one you know well, but certainly not someone you love nor cer-
> tainly not someone you hate. Just someone of whom you really
> do know quite a bit. Now come to some conclusions about him,
> impartially objective conclusions; describe him as if you were fur-
> nishing a report upon him for an identification to be made by an

F.B.I. agent who had never seen him. Write down his physical characteristics from memory, then consider his type, his customary behavior, his personal idiosyncracies. Check the next time you see him. Are his eyes really hazel, or would you now call them blue? Is that habit of his of scratching his ear really a habit by which the agent may recognize him or have you given it prominence only because it annoys you? When you have the description in such shape that you honestly believe it would serve as an identification, try it on someone else who knows him; see if it works and if that second can put the correct name upon the description you have funished. If you succeed in this, you have done well.

Now turn upon yourself in the same way. We will suppose your name is Smith; now let us see how recognizably you can describe Smith, as formerly you were describing Jones. Do not get lost in speculations as to who "you" are and what "your" connection with Smith may be. This is perfectly straightforward, perfectly rational, perfectly practical; you are simply considering Smith as anyone else might consider him, who is taking the trouble to come to confirmable conclusions and judgements concerning Smith and who is furnishing a written identification of him. It is important that you write it down, for that will, partially, prevent mere daydreaming.[6]

In addition to focusing on oneself as one is to others (which could be intensified with the use of film or videotape) it is also useful to review one's life, to take an impartial longitudinal study. The healing potential of telling oneself one's own story is honored in the practice of psychotherapy—its magical benefits are described in a Sufi teaching story in which a hungry and exhausted old woodcutter unwittingly attracts higher forces to his aid through a recital of his own story:

...It was too cold, and he was too hungry, to sleep. So he decided to tell himself, as if in a story, everything that had happened to him since his little daughter had first said that she wanted a different kind of food.

As soon as he had finished his story, he thought he heard another voice, saying, somewhere above him, out of the dawn, "Old man, what are you doing sitting there?"

"I am telling myself my own story," said the woodcutter.

"And what is that?" said the voice.

The old man repeated his tale. "Very well," said the voice. And then the voice told the woodcutter to close his eyes and to mount, as it were, a step. "But I do not see any step," said the old man. "Never mind, but do as I say," said the voice.

The old man did as he was told. As soon as he had closed his eyes he found that he was standing up and as he raised his right foot he felt that there was something like a step under it ...[7]

Gurdjieff gave the task to each of the members of his early Russian group to report on their whole lives from the beginning without suppressing anything. He spoke of this autobiography as "one of the first tests on the way," a prerequisite for further progress. To study one's life it is useful to make an organized attempt to recall the important, to de-emphasize the trivial, and to commit oneself to telling the story aloud, for the tones and overtones of the delivery can tell much about the degree of truth or falsity moment by moment.

Actually, looking at oneself from the point of view of another or in the context of one's personal history is useful and interesting —and yet not quite at the heart of the matter, which is to experience oneself here and now, moment by moment, impartially witnessing all manifestations as they occur. It is possible, even in the dulled state of inattention that is the ordinary human condition, to catch glimpses of one's characteristic activities such as gaits, postures, tones of voice. The data amassed through repeated, though brief, moments of self-observation may be used to understand the concept of many "I's" as it applies to one's own life, to study the relative activity of centers, to watch the ways in which energy leaks away in the course of every day, to detect the presence of buffers. As de Ropp puts it:

> What, then, is the beginning? It is simple. Accept the truth about the third state—accept multiplicity. There is, in fact, no I. There is a multitude. He who knows this ceases even to think of himself as I. He speaks of "it" or "this." Meanwhile he observes how different "I's" come and go—actors in his personal theater. Something new develops in him. One who observes. In one part of his being, this man is becoming objective toward himself. In one part of his being, he has ceased to lie. Insofar as he has ceased to lie, he is becoming liberated. The Observer combines objectivity with discrimination. The Observer knows who is who in the jungle. The Observer is the forerunner of the Master.[8]

Paradoxically, the gathering of observations, though it may take years and years, takes no time at all since it can be done right in the midst of life's activities.

As the process of getting to know oneself proceeds from the observation of bodily habits to the observation of emotional reactions and patterns of thinking, moments of self remembering— flashes of a higher level of consciousness—may occur and in time may become more frequent and lucid. Nicoll describes the process: *"Self-Remembering* is the most important thing of all and has many degrees and stages. Everyone can, to a limited degree, begin

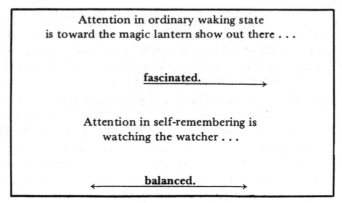

to practice and understand Self-Remembering. Full Self-Remembering is one thing, but many degrees exist in the approach to it."[9]

Self-remembering is not merely the observation of self, though that is difficult enough: it has a quality of attention that is unmistakable though difficult to convey, just as the taste of salt would be almost impossible to describe to someone who had never tasted it, but once known is easily recognized thereafter. This peculiar sensation is that of delivering to oneself the first conscious shock. Tracol asserts that "whether or not it be active in me, the possibility is given to me to become aware, at certain moments, of my own presence: I, here, now. This, when I experience it, is accompanied by a strangely familiar taste, a particular sensation that might be called 'genuinely' subjective. It is, quite simple, I. I recognize myself. I remember myself. I."[10]

During moments of self-remembering, attention is divided between the surrounding environment and one's inner self. Perceptions are clear and undistorted, both interiorly and exteriorly. Moments of self-remembering do occur gratuitously in life: most of what is remembered vividly is recorded during these flashes. The deliberate attempt to produce such moments, to sustain them and deepen them, is the backbone of the first line of work. At first there will be help in the form of structured practices:

> For primary exercises in self-remembering the participation of
> all three centers is necessary . . . At the beginning all three need
> to be evoked artificially. In the case of thought the means of
> artificially evoking them is conversations, lectures and so on. For
> example, if nothing is said, nothing is evoked. Readings, talks,
> have served as an artificial shock. I call it artificial because I was
> not born with these desires, they are not natural, they are not an
> organic necessity. These desires are artificial and their conse-
> quences will be equally artificial.

If thoughts are artificial, then I can create in myself sensations which are also artificial.

I repeat: artificial things are necessary only in the beginning. The fullness of what we desire cannot be attained artificially, but, for the beginning, this way is necessary.[11]

Along with efforts at self-observation and self-remembering there can be a parallel attempt to extend and deepen self-understanding through active interventions carried out on a small scale. It is possible to change certain aspects of overt behavior and to use such changes as reminders for flagging attention. Minor variations in the way habitual actions are carried out—as, for example, when a cigarette is held in the unaccustomed hand or the normal pace of walking is speeded up or slowed down—may foster significant improvement in the general level of awareness. Great caution must be used in making changes in habits since, as Gurdjieff repeatedly pointed out, the organism is a delicately balanced mechanism and any modification in one habit always brings about a corresponding adjustment in some other manifestation. This adjustment is often unpredictable and sometimes quite unwelcome.

Efforts to remember oneself during the day are sustained through a connection with a state of quiet meditation before the activity of daily life begins each morning. At first this period of sitting will involve only a sequence of physical relaxations and the enhancement of a general awareness of the body through focused attention to physical sensations: "For consciousness, attention is necessary. Attention is as oil in the lamp. Consciousness is the light."[12] As the student progresses, many techniques, all predicated on the assumption that a firm foundation in sensing the body has been established, are introduced. Sometimes the technique of bare attention is used in this period of quiet sitting; at others a question such as "Who am I?" is used as the object of contemplation.

If it were not the case that people in the Gurdjieff work sit in straight backed chairs in the Western manner—if we were to look only at technique—they would be hard to distinguish from Vipassana meditators as they do their silent morning practice. The concerns and methods are similar to (and perhaps derived from) the bare attention fundamental in Buddhist practice. The mind is typically full of chatter and activity at first, defying all attempts to allow interior silence and simple attention to sensation. As identification with the contents of mind lightens there may be some moments of clear consciousness. As meditation deepens it can serve as a point of reference for moments of self-remembering during active life and they, too, can become stronger and more reliable.

As the effects of self-remembering accumulate, so does the knowledge of one's various manifestations. Patterns begin to emerge that produce the kind of heat and light that are characteristic of the struggle between essence and personality. Nicoll describes one of the many stages in this process:

> The side of what we actually are, and the side of what we pretend and imagine we are, are two contradictory sides. These two contradictory sides, however, exist in everyone without exception. The action of the Work, once it is beginning to be wished for, makes us become gradually aware of this contradiction—over many years. Then we begin to have traces of real suffering—interspersed with all sorts of attempts at self-justifying and excuses and reactions—until we become, by inner taste, sick of self-justifying, excuses and so on. This marks a stage in the Work, a definite point in self-development.[13]

Gurdjieff put this sort of experience in its theoretical context:

> Here again the law of three works. Between the positive and the negative principles there must be friction, suffering. Suffering leads to the third principle. It is a hundred times easier to be passive so that suffering and results happen outside and not inside you. Inner result is achieved when everything takes place inside you.[14]

As self understanding develops there must arise a clearer and clearer conception of personal aim. Commitment to the "voluntary labor and intentional suffering" involved in the Gurdjieff work must increase as friction between essence and personality increases or else a person will become unwilling to endure the attendant pain. A personal aim may be felt in many ways. It is an individual matter. For one it is: "I wish to be master of myself," while for another it is: "I wish to be able to do good." However stated, it represents the level of a person's understanding, his or her orientation in working. It is against this aim that all other motives, actions and impulses must now be measured and upon which a new sense of morality is founded, for what aids my inner work is now deemed good and what does not must fall away. This attitude of "conscious egoism" marks a new phase of development. Gurdjieff once gave this exercise to a group:

> For those of you who are already able to remember your aim automatically, but have no strength to do it: Sit for a period of at least one hour alone. Make all your muscles relaxed. Allow your associations to proceed but do not be absorbed by them. Say to them: If you will let me do as I wish now, I shall later grant your wishes. Look on your associations as though they belonged to someone else, to keep yourself from identifying with them.

> At the end of an hour take a piece of paper and write your aim
> on it. Make this paper your God. Everything else is nothing. Take
> it out of your pocket and read it constantly, every day. In this
> way it becomes part of you, at first theoretically, later actually.
> To gain energy, practice this exercise of sitting still and making
> your muscles dead. Only when everything in you is quiet after an
> hour, make your decision about your aim. Don't let associations
> absorb you. To undertake a voluntary aim, and to achieve it, gives
> magnetism and the ability to 'do.'[15]

The most serious difficulty in remembering one's aim is the
plurality, inconsistency and fragmentation that characterize the
volitional situation of a person with many "I's." Yet although
there are many "I's" each person has one central attribute, a pillar
on which the personality structure rests or around which it could
be said to revolve. This "chief feature" is almost always invisible
to one oneself but other people can often give accurate enough information about it. Nicknames are often telling clues to chief
features.

Although hints and other aids are given the student, it is typically his or her task alone to determine what chief feature is by
piecing together the data collected in self observation. Sometimes
the teacher informs his disciple, as Thomas de Hartmann describes:

> From the first days, Mr. Gurdjieff had spoken with us about
> this chief weakness. To see it and to realize it is very painful, some-
> times unbearable. In esoteric schools, as I have mentioned, when
> the chief weakness is made clear to a man, it is revealed with great
> care, because the truth about himself can sometimes bring a man
> to such despair that he might end his life. A spiritual tie with the
> Teacher prevents such a tragedy. Holy Scripture speaks of the mo-
> ment of realizing one's chief defect when it says that when you are
> struck on the right cheek you must turn the left one. The pain of
> discovering your chief defect is like the shock of receiving a slap in
> the face. A man must find in himself the strength not to run away
> from this pain, but boldly to turn the other cheek; that is, to lis-
> ten and accept further truth about himself.[16]

Once chief feature is known it can provide the key to the invalida-
tion of personality so that essence is relatively stronger in its struggle
against it. In relating Gurdjieff's presentation of their chief features
to people in his group, Ouspensky described this incident:

> "There cannot be proper outward considering while a man is
> seated in his chief feature," said G. "For instance So-and-So" (he
> named one of our party). "His feature is that he is *never at home*.
> How can he consider anything or anybody? . . ."
> To another in our party he said on the question of feature that

his feature was that *he did not exist at all.*

"You understand, *I do not see you.*" said G. "It does not mean that you are always like that. But when you are like you are now, you do not exist at all."

He said to another that his chief feature was a tendency always to argue with everybody about everything.

"*But then I never argue.*" the man very heatedly at once replied. Nobody could help laughing.[17]

As self-study brings to light the facts about one's actual functioning and personality is, to some extent, seen through, it loses some of its stranglehold on essence and loses some of its force. It is no longer quite so believable: identification is no longer inevitably present. Work that requires a certain degree of self-control begins to be possible, and this includes work in relationship with other people, the second line of work.

THE SECOND LINE OF WORK

"The hardest thing for a man," said Gurdjieff, "is to endure the manifestations of others."[18] The second line of work provides special conditions and support in the effort to become aware of one's ways of relating to other people, and opportunities to practice new ways of being with others.

Just as habitual reactions of the physical body can become the subject of detailed study, patterns of emotional reaction can undergo observation and analysis. They have been the target of psychoanalytic investigation since its inception. The Gurdjieff work differs radically from psychotherapy, growth groups, and other aspects of the human potential movement, however, in its insistence that negative emotions are entirely unnecessary and we may suppress their outward expression (although observing them internally) without danger of provoking an unwanted compensatory adjustment in some other habit pattern. The suppression of negative emotions is preparatory to work on the second conscious shock. Thus for those who have undertaken the practice of self-remembering, the non-expression of negative emotions (which even a relatively superficial survey will show to be the vast majority of all emotional experiences ordinarily felt in daily life) will eventually be required. Nicoll talks about the process in its inception:

> I will remind you of the first step—namely, we are not asked to like, but to stop dislike and all its ramifications. This makes a very practical starting point. Later, when you feel the presence of a negative emotion in you as a foreign substance, as acutely as a stomach-ache, then you will seek, for your own reasons to work on yourself and transform your inner state for your own inner health.[19]

Suppressing the outward manifestation of negative emotions is an immensely difficult task, one which intensifies the struggle between essence and personality in ways that are often acutely painful. "To endure the manifestations of others is a big thing." Gurdjieff emphasized. "The last thing for a man. Only a perfect man can do this. Start by making your aim or your God the ability to bear one manifestation of one person that you cannot now endure without nervousness. If you 'wish' you 'can.' Without 'wishing' you never 'can.' Wish is the most powerful thing in the world. With conscious wish everything comes."[20]

As essence matures, standardized affective patterns acquired from parents and teachers become weaker: in Freudian terms, the control of superego diminishes. True feelings begin to appear, changing the quality of emotion for others and for oneself. Conscious wishes become possible and prayer may then be a possibility. According to Nicoll the signs of raising the emotional life to a higher plane include "a change in the feeling of 'I' " and "the ability to control lower emotion."[21] Going back to the metaphor of the carriage, the horse, the driver and the passenger:

> We must understand the difference between a casual passenger and the master of the cart. "I" is the master, if we have an "I." If we have not, there is always someone sitting in the cart and giving orders to the driver. Between the passenger and the driver there is a substance which allows the driver to hear. Whether these substances are there or not depends on many accidental things. It may be absent. If the substance has accumulated, the passenger can give orders to the driver, but the driver cannot order the horse, and so on. At times you can, at others you cannot, it depends on the amount of substance there is. Tomorrow you can, today you cannot. This substance is the result of many things.
>
> One of these substances is formed when we suffer. We suffer whenever we are not mechanically quiet. There are different kinds of suffering. For instance, I want to tell you something, but I feel it is best to say nothing. One side wants to tell, the other wants to keep quiet. The struggle produces a substance. Gradually this substance collects in a certain place.[22]

When people gather together for any reason the opportunities to suffer in this way increase. Gurdjieff even provoked it. Fritz Peters describes how Gurdjieff actually paid one man, "who without conscious effort, produced friction in all the people around him, to live at the Prieure."[22] The Gurdjieff work continues this form of help by encouraging collaboration in many kinds of physical labor and arts and crafts projects that groups undertake. During these periods of work together personalities inevitably clash. Sometimes special tasks are given that act as attention sharpeners or dividers as, for example, counting forward and backward in various patterns while working. External considering, which may be thought of as a fundamental exercise in the practice of love, provides further information about patterns of emotional function, as the attempt to relate in this way throws the paranoia and self-centeredness of personality into strong relief. If the suffering entailed is strong enough the crust of conscience, lying dormant in the less-than-conscious part of each human being, may be uncovered to give a glimpse, however brief, of what real morality—apart from cultural traditions or mores—might be.

External considering is responding as the other wants or needs without inward identification. Only one who is relatively conscious can play a tune on those he or she meets, rather than reacting helplessly to the world.

> The work needs nothing external. Only the internal is needed. Externally, one should play a role in everything. Externally, a man should be an actor, otherwise he does not answer the requirements of life. One man likes one thing; another, another thing: if you want to be a friend to both and behave in one way, one of them will not like it; if you behave in another way, the other will not like it. You should behave with one as he likes it and with the other as this other likes it. Then your life will be easier.[24]

Ordinary people act as they are dictated from inside. The awakened act in choiceless awareness of what is appropriate to the situation. Personal history, upon which all negativity is based, is seen through as though transparent and the energy released is available for use as the second conscious shock—completing the assimilation of food, air and impressions that marks the evolved human being.

THE THIRD LINE OF WORK

The first line of work might be thought of as self-centered, as an individual concentrates on personal process to gain awareness and increase the level of being. The second line of work involves relationship, interaction with other people, but still the attention is focused on individual patterns of reaction to others and to the social context. In both the first and the second lines of work the indications of a teacher are followed. In the third line of work, which is work done for the benefit of the ideas of the work itself, initiative is allowed and even encouraged and personal growth or gain is not the main thrust of effort.

In the third line of work, the needs and requirements of the

THE HARMONIOUS DEVELOPMENT OF THE HUMAN BEING[25]

Being complete in oneself and independent of outside shocks, the perfected being embodies the *Seal of Solomon*.

With the pentagram locked within—that is, with centers permanently in accord—the physically perfect human being is brought into contact with the higher centers which introduce the missing principle and effect a direct and permanent connection with objective consciousness.

Bringing the work of all five centers into harmony is one of the meanings of *the construction of the pentagram.*

△

Strengthening the decision to work toward consciousness and against mechanicality and bringing this decision into all events that were formerly accidental produces a permanent line of results in time, *transforming the trinity into fourfoldness.*

△

The creation of *a permanent third principle, the struggle for consciousness,* transforms duality into trinity. A definite decision is made to work against mechanicalness, based on recognition of one's condition.

△

The ordinary human being is a duality: all one's experiences are divided into opposites. Everything is divided. Through self-deceit one sees what is mechanical as conscious and what is divided as single and whole.

---

organization, the group of people who have come together to work on themselves, are considered. Selfless service is the heart of the third line of work, and since any selfless action is beyond the capacity of human beings in the ordinary levels of consciousness, this line of work cannot involve any sustained effort until personality is, at least to some degree, disarmed and the level of consciousness improved.

THE MOVEMENTS

The rhythmic gymnastic movements and dances that Gurdjieff adapted from Asiatic sources for use in the work have the twofold purpose of conveying a certain kind of knowledge and offering the means for attaining a harmonious state of being. They are a kind of meditation in action that also has the properties of an

(Text continues on page 88.)

The Enneagram　　　　1.　　　　　　　　　　4.　　　　　　　　　　2.

GURDJIEFF MOVEMENTS: Basic positions of two of
the many sacred dances Gurdjieff brought from the East.
The movements are performed rhythmically with musical
accompaniment.

photo permission: Joseph Camhi

Number 17

　　　　　　　　　1.　　　　　　　　　　2.　　　　　　　　　　3.

8.   5.   7.

4.   5.   6.

From "The Fifth Obligatory Exercise."

GROUP PERFORMING GURDJIEFF MOVEMENTS UNDER THE AUTHOR'S DIRECTION

photos: Ernest Lowe

Intermets from a dance called "Lord Have Mercy."

From "The Six Positions"—this is the second.

From "The First Obligatory Exercise."

art form and a language. The body of Gurdjieff movements consists of many different kinds of dances: there are six obligatory exercises to be learned by everyone; dervish dances requiring toughness and endurance for men only; soft and beautiful dances for women; prayers in motion with complex and symbolic choreography; dances in which there is a spoken element such as "Lord Have Mercy!" or "Mother, Father, Sister, Brother"; slow and reverent dances and incredibly precise and active dances. Their sources include Turkestan, Tibet, Afghanistan, Kafirstan, Chitral, Chian, Transcaspia and Turkey.

In practicing these movements an effort is made to divide the attention and remember oneself, for often the head, arms, hands and feet must follow different beats and without a certain level of awareness performing them well is quite impossible. Right working of centers and consistent attention are involved in doing the movements correctly. One moment of inattention, one error, may involve the loss of an elaborate count and render the dancer unable to deny a lapse of awareness.

The Gurdjieff movements are a unique contribution to the resources of those who are able, to some extent at least, to meditate while sitting still and quiet and who are ready to extend their state of recollected attention to a more active milieu. They are done to music, which engages the emotional center in the effort of the intellectual center to follow the indicated patterns and of the moving-instinctive level of function to go against all personal and idiosyncratic biases in performing unusual postures and gestures.

Lifelong conditioning locks each individual into his or her own repertoire of thoughts, feelings and physical attitudes. In ordinary waking state each kind of thought is inevitably connected with a certain kind of emotional tone and a certain way of holding the body. Given one, the others follow. The number of postures, gaits, gestures is, furthermore, quite limited: the typical adult is very unlikely to enter into any new and non-habitual postures and therefore just as unlikely to experience any unfamiliar emotional states, nor altered states of consciousness, unless something is done to break the vicious circle. Contemporary psychological thought has noticed this: Reichian vegetotherapy, bioenergetics, the Alexander technique, and Rolfing are some of the ways developed to release the physical body from its conditioned constraints, thus enlarging and enriching intellectual and emotional possibilities. The Feldenkreis system, first publicly demonstrated at the Gurdjieff center in Coombe Springs, England, is another.

The Gurdjieff movements break the cycle by requiring that

the dancer move in non-natural and non-habitual ways seldom
seen in normal life: the right arm and leg may move in unison, for
example, or the eyes turn in a direction opposite that of the head.
In each of the movements the usual modes of physical expression
are challenged and a new freedom may come into being.

All our movements are automatic; most are unconscious. Because we can never change the repertoire of thinking and feeling
without changing the repertoire of postures, and since by the very
nature of the requirement for attention to what is unconscious a
person cannot easily break this pattern alone, but only with outside help, some Sufi orders use the "Stop!" exercise in which everything instantly freezes at the master's command. Gurdjieff used
this method as well as the movements for studying physical manifestations.

> A non-mechanical study of oneself is only possible with the
> help of the "stop" exercise under the direction of a man who un-
> derstands it.
>
> Let us try to follow what occurs. A man is walking, or sitting,
> or working. At that moment he hears a signal. A movement that
> has begun is interrupted by this sudden signal or command to stop.
> His body becomes immovable and arrested *in the midst of a tran-
> sition from one posture to another, in a position in which he nev-
> er stays in ordinary life.* Feeling himself in this state, that is, in an
> unaccustomed posture, a man involuntarily looks at himself from
> new points of view, sees and observes himself in a new way. In
> this unaccustomed posture he is able to think in a new way, feel
> in a new way, know himself in a new way. In this way the circle
> of old automatism is broken. The body tries in vain to adopt an
> ordinary comfortable posture. But the man's will, brought into
> action by the will of the teacher, prevents it.[26]

Gurdjieff demonstrated the "Stop!" exercise in his earliest visit to
America, in 1924, to large audiences. Its use today in Gurdjieff
groups is limited by the requirement that it be used only by a
teacher who has a level of mastery allowing complete empathy with
each pupil in each position for otherwise it can be dangerous to
nerves and blood vessels. The movements carry less risk.

In addition to their value in the study of physical manifestation, the movements are said to be a form of objective art. Objective art comes from conscious sources and produces its intended effects on participants and audiences without variation—or with variation dependent only upon level of personal development. Like
some Balinese and Indonesian dance forms, the movements often
represent a kind of bodily semaphore or symbolic method of communication. Each position has its own meaning and presumably can

TWO KINDS OF ART

Objective	Subjective
Conscious.	Unconscious.
An artist creates it, knowing what he or she is doing and why.	It is created.
It makes an identical impression on everybody and produces the same definite reactions, with variation depending only on level of personal development.	It acts on people according to associations.
It contains exactly what the artist wants.	What it contains depends on accident only.
Its purpose is the illumination of truth through the emotional experience of the recipient.	Its purpose is the expression of the "self" of the artist.
Its origin is at least flashes of objective consciousness, utilized with unity and control by the artist.	Its origin is the associations of the artist.
Possible examples: the Great Pyramid, the early Gothic cathedrals of Notre Dame, Rheims and Chartres, snake charmers' music which works with "inner octaves" of one sustained note, the ancient statue of Zeus at Olympus, the drama of the life of Jesus, the Twelve Acts of the Buddha.	Possible examples: All music, dance, painting, sculpture, poetry and prose that produce varied effects on people and do not have at least some of the intended effect on all. All works that do not originate from conscious sources.

be deciphered by those initiated into the code. Although the movements come from many sources, perhaps the chief of these is a hidden monastery in the Hindu Kush to which Gurdjieff was taken, and in which he saw priestess-dancers taught sacred temple dances using a most peculiar piece of equipment:

> The external appearance of these peculiar apparatuses gave the impression, at first glance, that they were of very ancient workmanship. They were made of ebony inlaid with ivory and mother-of-pearl. When they were not in use and stood grouped together, they reminded one of "Vasanelian" trees, with branches all alike. On close examination, we saw that each apparatus consisted of a smooth column, higher than a man, which was fixed on a tripod. From this column, in seven places, there projected specially designed branches, which in turn were divided into seven parts of different dimensions, each successive part decreasing in length and width in proportion to its distance from the main column . . .[27]

A more recent account of what must be the same monastery is given by Desmond Martin:

> An articulated tree, of gold and other metals, which seemed to me unbelievably beautiful and resembled a Babylonian work of art which I had seen in the Bagdad Museum, was by far the most impressive. It served to indicate the postures assumed by dervishes in their yoga-like exercises, which, performed to special music, they studied for self-development.[28]

The monastery was that of the Sarmoun Brotherhood, the Sufi order whose ideas of the materiality of knowledge and of universal laws may also be the source of the fundamental principles of Gurdjieff's cosmology.

THE ROLE OF PHYSICAL LABOR IN THE WORK

Contemporary people have lost the opportunity, especially if they are urban and educated, to engage in the kind of manual labor for which the human organism evolved. Real physical exertion helps centers to work as they were intended and to stop interfering with one another. This produces a chance for harmony. Therefore people who work on themselves according to the teachings of Gurdjieff create opportunities to do farm work, construction work, and other heavy tasks in order to normalize bodily functioning. There are some things that are possible for the body only when it is burdened with taxing requirements involving great attention and heavy energy expenditure under conditions of inadequate sleep. Under such stress the centers have no leeway to work wrongly. Furthermore, efforts made up to and beyond the point of exhaustion may permit access to a special reservoir of energy which Gurdjieff called the "large accumulator," as contrasted with the small, peripheral reservoirs of energy that are ordinarily available to draw upon:

> Small accumulators suffice for the ordinary, everyday work of life. But for work on oneself, for inner growth, and for efforts required of a man who enters the way, the energy from these small accumulators is not enough.
> We must learn to draw energy straight from the large accumulator.[29]

The large accumulator provides the "second wind" that comes when, spent from the tremendous effort of climbing a mountain or fighting off fatigue in tending the sick throughout the night, one suddenly feels an influx of energy and the strength to go on as if after a refreshing sleep. Although we naturally switch from one small accumulator to another in the course of a day or a night, switching to the large accumulator, which can happen only in great exhaustion, opens the possibility of making super-efforts, impossible in the ordinary state, which may, like the powerful first stage of a rocket, allow liberation from the laws that now bind us to the level of the earth.

EXPERIENTIAL EXERCISES

Work on oneself according to Gurdjieff's teachings is individual and empirical. Results are directly proportional to understanding. Nothing must be accepted unless it has been compellingly proved by personal experiment and, in fact, blind faith is not in accord with the basic orientation of the work. "No 'faith' is required on the fourth way; on the contrary, faith of any kind is opposed to the fourth way," Gurdjieff insisted. "On the fourth way a man must satisfy himself of the truth of what he is told. And until he is satisified he must do nothing."[30]

Consider the basic premise that consciousness as we know it in the ordinary waking state is very limited and inconsistent. Ouspensky gave this demonstration in a lecture:

> Take a watch and look at the second hand, *trying to be aware of yourself,* and concentrating on the thought, "I am Peter Ouspensky," "I am now here." Try not to think about anything else, simply follow the movements of the second hand and be aware of yourself, your name, your existence, and the place where you are. Keep all other thoughts away.
>
> You will, if you are persistent, be able to do this *for two minutes. This is the limit of your consciousness.* And if you try to repeat the experiment soon after, you will find it more difficult than the first time.[31]

A.R. Orage, who headed the Gurdjieff work in New York for many years, gave these additional instructions on another occasion:

> Now take another step. Keeping the focus as before, count mentally the numbers one to ten backwards, slowly, during the course of one revolution of the hand. This requires a double attention, as it were. You are observing the movement and counting deliberately at the same time. At first it may be easy, but do it again and again until it becomes difficult; and *then do it!* This is a very important piece of advice.[32]

This exercise can be made more and more complex until the limits of attention are clearly evident.

Because we have such inconsistent awareness, and because what we do have is so often distorted by identification, it may be difficult to conceive of the degree to which we react mechanically and are unable to act without reaction—to "do." It is necessary to take some distance from personal involvement in one's own life experience in order to truly be an impartial witness. Orage described a procedure for reviewing the events of a day that, when practiced regularly, ought to yield a great deal of information that would enrich the understanding of the notion of human mechanicality. Here is a condensed version of this technique:

Before going to sleep, begin to count slowly to yourself a series of simple numbers, backwards and forwards, such as 2, 4, 6, 8, 10—10, 8, 6, 4, 2. Continue this repetition rhythmically. Having got this rhythm moving, almost but never quite automatically, deliberately try to picture yourself as you appeared on getting up that morning.

You woke, you got out of bed, you proceeded to dress, to breakfast, to read the paper, to catch a bus and so on. Try to follow this sequence of yourself pictorially observed, from moment to moment, exactly as if you were unwinding a film. At first you will find the exercise difficult . . . the necessity to count continuously will trouble you at this stage. Nevertheless, continue; for the fact is that counting occupies the thinking brain and thus naturally allows the pictorial memory to work more easily. . . . Thinking not only impedes the pictorial representation but it subtly but surely falsifies the pictures.[33]

According to Orage, other difficulties that may be encountered are the interruptions due to failures in memory that everybody experiences and the likelihood that when thinking and worrying (the main components of the inner chatter that fills ordinary waking consciousness) cease or are drastically attenuated, sleep may put an end to the exercise before the day's review is complete.

If the nightly review of each day's activities is practiced consistently it may happen that moments of self-observation begin to occur spontaneously during the day. The locus of awareness may move up in time so that it occasionally appears in the here and now rather than in memory or anticipation. It is at this point that the collection of data on thinking, feeling and sensing functions may begin. Moments of self-observation, or "snapshots," may be taken of gestures, tones of voice, facial expressions, and ways of habitual interaction with others to form a collection in which the patterns of functioning that make each of us a recognizable individual can be discerned. As the details of mechanical functioning become clear from an extensive collection of these snapshots, wasteful and inefficient kinds of reaction will be identifiable and what to do about them (if anything) will perhaps be apparent. During each step of this process, progress must be based on an understanding that is so personal that it cannot be forgotten or denied. Al-Ghazali learned this the hard way when a brigand who stole everything from him, including his cherished lecture notes, declared, "Knowledge that can be stolen is not worth having."

But enough of this. Some self-study can be accomplished on one's own but as the Sufis say, "He who has no guide has Shaitan (the devil) as a guide." Observations made without the context of a teaching situation must inevtiably be subject to the falsifications Orage warned about; thinking mind is full of biases and tricks of distortion that make these biases look to oneself as if they were the pure truth. Exercises on one's own are fine for a preface but not for the body of the work.

I need hardly say much to you about the impor-
tance of authority. Only a very few civilized persons
are capable of existing without reliance on others
or are even capable of coming to an independent
opinion. You cannot exaggerate the intensity of
man's inner irresolution and craving for authority.
                                                —Sigmund Freud

The level of Gurdjieff's and Ouspensky's most de-
voted students was very high. In order to study this
movement, nobody will have to do any intellectual
slumming.

                                                —J.B. Priestley

          Look not at my exterior form,
          but take what is in my hand.
                        —Maulana Jelaluddin Rumi

CHAPTER SIX:
The Living Tradition

> After the death of a Master, what becomes of his disciples and the teaching he has transmitted to them? What kind of Master do we speak of here and what kind of disciple? If, when the bell tolls, a man's disciples inaugurate a cult, become sectarian, or fanatical, freeze his thought and codify his slightest utterance—can such a situation relate to a real Master?[1]

According to some it was Gurdjieff's failure that he never trained a single disciple who was capable of understanding what was expected of him. According to others the Gurdjieff tradition is still a living vine knowingly cultivated by those who understand the work and its meaning. Whatever the case may be, there are many Gurdjieff groups and their fruits can be tasted by those who really wish to do so.

THE GURDJIEFF FOUNDATIONS

In late October, 1949 in the American Hospital in Paris, the dying Gurdjieff spent long hours in a private interview with Jeanne de Salzmann who, with her late husband Alexander had been his student from the very early days in Tiflis and Constantinople. Since that time Mme. de Salzmann has served as the head of a network of Gurdjieff Foundations throughout the world. Certainly those who are bent on entering the Gurdjieff work should seriously consider trying to make contact with one of these Foundations. It can be done by writing to the publisher of Gurdjieff's works. Becoming part of one of the Gurdjieff Foundations generally involves participation in weekly group meetings. These are usually conducted by someone who was taught by someone who worked directly with Gurdjieff himself. The groups typically have a question-and-answer format: there is silence until someone asks a question and is answered by the group leader, and silence between questions. Students make the attempt to recollect themselves to bring every bit

GURDJIEFF'S TEACHINGS: SOME LINES OF TRANSMISSION

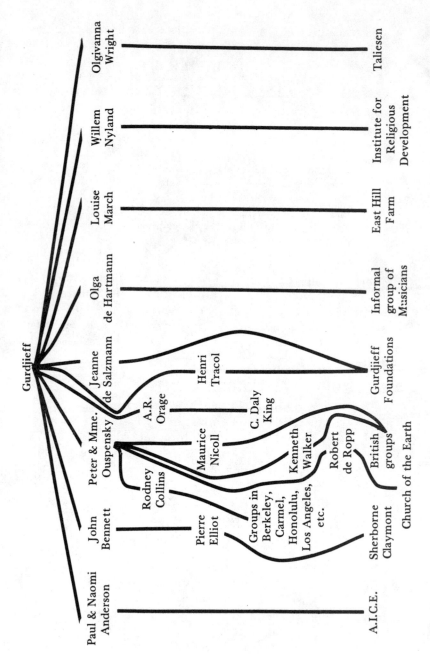

of their attention to bear on these questions and answers, which have to do with the practical aspects of self-study and the meaning of attempts at inner work. Because the topics for discussion arise from members of the group rather than the teacher or leader, the group receives just as much as its collective level of understanding indicates and no more.

It is usual that after a few months of discussion students are allowed to study the movements. In addition there may also be readings of Gurdjieff's works, published and unpublished, that are open to all members of all groups, and work days on the property or at some country retreat where small crews labor under the guidance of teachers and elder students.

Outside the network of Gurdjieff Foundations there are a growing number of groups—some 20 or so according to the New York Times—that present themselves as transmitting Gurdjieff's teachings. Some of these are like Protestant sects dissenting from what they feel is an atmosphere of frigid severity and nervous spiritual materialism within the Gurdjieff orthodoxy. Others have been formed by those with more goodwill and imagination than connection, direct or indirect, with Gurdjieff. As Gurdjieff pointed out, a teaching situation may be effective if the ideas come from conscious sources, even if the teacher cannot fully identify or specify their origin—thus some of these splinter groups may serve the function of acquainting seekers with the ideas of the work. Although all groups have their place in the scheme of things only those with a direct lineage and substantial impact will be considered here.

SHERBORNE AND CLAYMONT

The Gurdjieff Foundations have a combined membership that must number in the thousands. No other line of transmission has affected so many. Perhaps the next best known line is that of the late John Bennett and his students in England and America. Bennett first met Gurdjieff in Constantinople in 1921. He was one of the few who could converse with Gurdjieff in his native language. His connections with Gurdjieff lasted, on and off, until Gurdjieff's death in 1949. According to Bennett, Gurdjieff asked him to transmit his teaching to the world. This he did, though with some hesitation. After following various other spiritual pursuits for 20 years, Bennett founded the International Academy for Continuous Education at Sherborne House, a rambling Georgian mansion in the small town of Sherborne, Gloustershire, near Oxford, England. Bennett described the orientation of the Academy in a prospectus:

The Academy is an experiment based on the assumption that
every human being is born with the potential for self-realization
through self-education—after the automatic growing process is
substantially completed in the first twenty years of life. Man can
choose to continue to develop by his own conscious efforts and
this development will open doors at present closed to all but a
favored few. More and more people feel the need to step out of
the narrow image of man imposed by an educational system which
is designed to produce specialists, and intellectual specialists at
that. The aim of the Academy is to equip students with techniques
that they will be able to apply throughout their lives for more effective use of all their powers—bodily, mental and spiritual. The
ability to learn throughout life, to adapt and make independent
judgements will be increasingly necessary in the future. Social unrest throughout the world is in great measure due to the inability of
people to adapt to modern life because their education has failed
to show them how to live in a rapidly changing world. If mankind
is to enter a phase of conscious evolution, if our past is not to be
our future, then specific techniques of self-realization must be
available to all. If the Academy succeeds in its self-imposed task,
it may well be a precursor of similar instruments adapted to the
needs of a changing world. It is for people of both sexes, of all
ages, all races, intellectuals and non-intellectuals. There are only
two conditions for admission: a genuine wish to find out how to
live more effectively on all levels and a readiness to work hard to
find the answer.[2]

The training program as given in the prospectus is most ambi-
tious. It includes courses on Communication, Cosmology, Energies,
Commitment and Decision, Gurdjieff and the Masters of Wisdom,
Human Types, Psychology, Gurdjieff Movement Exercises, Human
Body, Hazards and the Failure of Human Purpose, Role Playing,
Group Dynamics, Authentic Science, Creative Thinking, Self Expression, Group Decision Making, Drama, Music and the Emotions,
many of them taught by Bennett himself. In the five years from its
inception in 1971 until the last group of students left in 1975 after
Bennett's death, several hundred people participated in a ten month
residential training program based on Gurdjieff's teachings at Sherborne.

As many of the students at Sherborne had been recruited in
an American speaking tour conducted by Bennett in 1971, and he
had already made plans to found a branch in the United States, it
was natural that after his death the focus of the work he had begun
should migrate westward to America. Thus, in another rambling
mansion, this time in the Shenandoah Valley of West Virginia, a
new residential training program, based on Bennett's version of the

Gurdjieff work, was posthumously born. The Claymont Society School for Continuous Education made this offering in its prospectus:

> Those who are already convinced that transformation is possible and know that nothing else gives meaning to life, are in search of methods of achieving it that really work. Those who are aware that there is something terribly wrong with the way human life on this earth is going—and especially their own lives—are looking for a way out. The School has something to offer them and all those who feel the need to help their fellow men and know that they must first help themselves.[3]

The long term aims of Claymont Society are described in the prospectus as the development of a Fourth Way School and the establishment of a model society that is self-sufficient and satisfying on all planes: physical, intellectual and spiritual. As it is in its first year of life at the time of this writing, there is no way to assess the degree of its effectiveness in fostering individual development and social change.

TALIESIN

Another line of transmission culminated in a school of architecture, The Taliesin Fellowship in Spring Green, Wisconsin where Frank Lloyd Wright and his wife, Olgivanna, directed a community along lines inspired by Gurdjieff. Olgivanna Wright had lived at the Prieure and had accompanied Gurdjieff and 25 pupils to New York in 1924 where they demonstrated the movements and instructed work groups. Later that year she met Frank Lloyd Wright at the Chicago Opera. She married him four years later. It was she who introduced Wright to the ideas of Gurdjieff, and she who provided the work orientation and discipline at Taliesin. When they opened the doors of Taliesin to the first students in 1932, Olgivanna was 34 and Frank Lloyd Wright was already a grand old man of 65.

> The place was run as a fellowship—"The Taliesen Fellowship" under the direction of Mr. and Mrs. Frank Lloyd Wright, whose aim was to produce an organic architecture in an organic life; the idea being, that to bring about an organic state of society men and women must begin by living a three-fold life, a life simultaneously of the instincts, the feelings and the mind. Their feet must be firmly planted on the earth and they must be able to use their hands; they must be able to appreciate the things of the feelings—music, poetry, painting and so on; and they must be able to think. This three-fold activity gave the place an extraordinary vitality. It was a real architectural school, in which the pupils lived with the Master, who taught them that if they wished to design

houses they must also be able to build with their own hands, to know the feel of the materials they worked with.[4]

Gurdjieff and Wright first met in June, 1931, after Gurdjieff had given a lecture in Chicago. Wright was impressed. He wrote of Gurdjieff that he seemed to "have the stuff in him of which our genuine prophets have been made. And when the prejudice against him has cleared away his vision of truth will be recognized as fundamental . . ."[5] Gurdjieff again visited the Wrights in 1936, this time after the students had come to Taliesin and he impressed everyone with his cooking and his presence. Wright proposed to send some of his apprentices to France to work with Gurdjieff.

" 'Then they can come back to me and I'll finish them off.'

" 'You finish!' Gurdjieff flashed, 'You are idiot. *You* finish! No! *You* begin. I finish.' "[6]

Though no student exchanges of this sort did take place, the orientation of Taliesin toward Gurdjieff's ideas remained strong. Fritz Peters reported:

> There is no question but that Olgivanna "ran" Taliesen West like a transplanted Prieure, even down to the architectural students wearing the same "costumes" that Gurdjieff students sometimes wore for so-called demonstrations of dances and/or movements.[7]

Whether Taliesin was an imitation or a genuine offspring of Gurdjieff's method, when the Wrights were there it was a functioning community in which the influence of Gurdjieff's spirit was certainly present. Yet nothing stays still. Taliesin is still in existence but what was in it of Gurdjieff work may have gone down the octave, as is the nature of all processes that do not increase in force.

THE CHURCH OF THE EARTH

Robert S. de Ropp, a student of Mr. and Mme. Ouspensky and, briefly, of Gurdjieff himself, leads a Gurdjieff community in Sonoma County, California. This group has attempted to become a self-sustaining alternative society by farming the land and the sea, making the conscious choice to come directly under the laws governing the biosphere, as a personal and specific recognition of mankind's place in the ray of creation. It is called the Church of the Earth. De Ropp writes:

> Wake up, open your eyes, hear, smell, feel, taste, touch, become alive. You cannot afford to pass your life in sleep. All around you, ceaselessly at work, are the forces which generate and sustain your life. How can you afford to be blind to these great forces, to wander through life in a dream like the Fool in

the Tarot, so asleep that he does not even know that he's losing
his pants? The cosmic drama is displayed before you every hour
of the day. An endless series of transformations, seeds to plants,
flowers to fruits, plants to animals, refuse to soil, takes place before your eyes. Every plant, every animal, the clouds, the sun, the
ocean, can tell you stories about itself if you will only listen. By
learning to see, by learning to hear, by stopping dreams, and by
awakening you become what man is supposed to be, the eyes and
ears of the god, or if you prefer, a part of the consciousness of the
cosmos.

This aim, this struggle to awaken, is the basis of the true religious impulse. All the other manifestations of religion, the dog-
mas and rituals, the myths and fairy stories, the threats of damna-
tion and dreams of heaven are merely aspects of the world's old-
est con game, invented by paid priests to separate the fools from
their money. As for our Church of the Earth, we have no paid
priests. We have teachers who know certain things, and their mot-
to is plain,
I cannot teach that which I do not know.[8]

At the present time the community, which was dreamed of as
a new Garden of Eden watered by a stream purer than the American mainstream, is lying fallow. The group is small and through a
quirk of fate, landless. Whether de Ropp will be willing to take new
students is an open question.

EAST HILL FARM

Another Gurdjieff community, East Hill Farm in Middlesex,
New York is a self-sustaining group of artisans and farmers whose
wares of clay, glass, iron, wood and wool are marketed in the name
of Rochester Folk Guild. This group is directed by Louise March,
an artist herself who was with Gurdjieff at the Prieure and who was
connected with the Gurdjieff Foundation in New York for many
years before starting the Rochester Folk Guild in 1957. She
founded East Hill Farm ten years later. According to the *New
York Times:*

> There is a self-contained, self-absorbed almost monastic qual-
> ity about the life on this farm. In the fields and workshops, the
> craftsmen labor, sometimes long into the night, seldom speaking
> except to respond to a question or give a direction. Only the old
> railroad bell that calls them to meals breaks the quiet.
> They cultivate silence, they say, "so that the activity of the
> hands harmonizes with that of the thoughts and feelings."[9]

The community is made up of about 40 people who work to master their crafts and themselves as they are "chiselled and molded"
by their teacher.

used by permission: Eleanor Beckham

photo: Ron Chamberlain

**upper left: portrait of Mme.
de Salzmann**
upper right: Wm. Nyland
lower left: Louise March & student

photo: N.Y. Times

A.I.C.E.

The Conway Gurdjieff group, also known as the "Anderson Group," is incorporated as the American Institute for Continuing Education. It has connected groups in other areas. Conway is situated in a beautiful fertile valley in the Berkshires. Though the property itself is not large, it has both a kitchen garden and a larger garden for other crops, several outbuildings, a large house which serves for many activities (as well as housing those who live on the premises) and a cottage, which serves as a residence, an office, and a guest house.

The Conway Group is composed of a spectrum of people, most of whom live in the contiguous towns and villages. There are artists, as well as artisans, construction people, maintenance and farm hands as well as foresters and landscapers, business people, bankers and accountants, linguists, and many students, undergraduates and graduates. There is indeed a diversity of types.

This group is under the guidance of Paul and Naomi Anderson, both long-time Gurdjieff students, whose beginnings date back to the original Orage Group. Paul Anderson was a resident at the Institute for the Harmonious Development of Man, in the period after Gurdjieff's accident, when only Americans were allowed to come. The Andersons also jointly put out the first English version of *All and Everything*, a mimeographed copy. It was published in 1930–31 for the purpose of raising funds for Gurdjieff. Both Andersons were members during the dissolution by Gurdjieff of the Orage Group.

During the mid-Thirties, the Andersons lived in Washington, D.C., where Gurdjieff visited them, bringing as he said all his "Writings" with him. These he made available to be read at their group meetings in Washington. In 1948–49, his last visit to America, he appointed Paul Anderson to be his "American Secretary" as well as one of the two co-representatives handling his public relations.

After his death in France in 1949, the Andersons participated in the activities of the newly-formed Gurdjieff Foundation in New York. After some years, the Andersons voluntarily left to follow what Gurdjieff had earlier confirmed that they should do, namely, to establish their own groups.

THE INSTITUTE FOR RELIGIOUS DEVELOPMENT

The students of the late Willem Nyland continue to operate a farm and various cottage industries in Warwick, New York after the death of their teacher in 1975. Willem Nyland, a Dutch chemist and serious musician, studied with Orage and Gurdjieff and was part

of the Gurdjieff Foundation of New York until the early 1960s
when he broke away to form his own group. Initially a New York
City-based discussion group, the circle of his students expanded to
include several discussion groups and movements groups on the
East and West coasts and two rural communities, one in Warwick,
New York and another in Sebastopol, California.

MME. DE HARTMANN'S GROUP

Olga de Hartmann presently lives in a desert community in
the Southwest where a group of musicians and friends gather around
her for occasional discussions and movements sessions. Most of Mme.
de Hartmann's work centers around the music that her late husband,
Thomas de Hartmann, composed on his own and in collaboration
with Gurdjieff. There is a large body of this music, some of which
has been painstakingly hand-copied by Mme. de Hartmann, published, and recorded. The performers of the de Hartmann and
Gurdjieff musical legacy are often sent to Mme. de Hartmann for
coaching before concerts, for in her sounds the living heart of
Gurdjieff's teachings.

OTHER GROUPS

These are not the only groups authentically connected with
Gurdjieff—some of those with long training in the work are leading
small private groups on their own. Others who never knew Gurdjieff but whose orientation is so similar that the same sources seem
to be present in them include E.J. Gold's Institute for the Harmonious Development of the Human Being in Crestline, California,
and Oscar Ichazo's Arica Institutes. A student of a student of
Rodney Collins teaches groups in various California cities. And an
architect from New York commutes to the Bay Area regularly to
conduct groups that are in the living tradition of the Gurdjieff work.
In addition to those affected directly by these groups, many more
are influenced indirectly through the diffusion of ideas into the culture via the works of artists, authors, poets, philosophers and scien-
tists on whom the teachings have had an impact.

There are many other groups that use the name of Gurdjieff,
and for all I can tell (having had the honor of knowing many but
not all of the early Gurdjieff people) there may be some that actually transmit his teaching. Many more do not. How can a person
who is seriously interested in joining the Gurdjieff work move wise-
ly among all these possible sources? Says de Ropp:

Even people who sincerely wish to transform themselves and
to assist in the transforming of others can lose their way because
of credulity, because they would rather believe blindly than test
things for themselves. All attempts, therefore, on the part of those
who have attained inner freedom, to liberate men from their bond-
age, tend to become frustrated by the credulity of man, coupled
with his laziness and reluctance to think for himself.

So, no matter how powerful the teacher, his followers can always be trusted to make a mishmash of his teachings and bring his
work to a halt. This they generally do by creating a cult of personality around the teacher himself, and fossilizing everything in
exactly the form in which it was given. Using this fossilized teaching they engage in mechanical repetitions of certain patterns of
behavior assuring themselves and each other that they will attain
liberation and higher consciousness as long as they never, never
make the slightest change in anything the master taught.

But life is change, and what is appropriate for one period is not
necessarily valid for another. So all this effort to hold onto certain forms only results in the arrest of development. So another
teacher has to appear, smash the fossil, start all over again. This,
of course, causes shrieks of indignation among the True Believers,
whose sleep is disturbed and whose comfortable habits are dis-
arranged.[10]

The form of the fourth way must depend on the time, the
place and the people. There is no hope of recognizing its authentic
manifestation by language, overt activity and purpose, or outward
appearance. Though perfect teachers exist, those in ordinary waking
state cannot see them. A search for the teaching will be an essay in
one's preconceptions, dependency needs and mechanical functioning, another turn on the endless circle of conditioning. How, then,
can the teaching be contacted?

According to Gurdjieff, the way to attract the right situation
is to collect and concentrate in one's own being higher substances,
higher vibrations which call to themselves the forces that are wait-
ing to help us. When the student is ready the teacher appears. This
is one meaning of the Biblical phrase, "To him who hath will it be
given; from him who hath not it will be taken away." The work of
gathering one's forces is the conscious effort of self-remembering
and the voluntary suffering of living in reality, here and now.

THE DIFFUSION OF FOURTH WAY TEACHING IN THE WEST:
culturally influential people who have been
affected by Gurdjieff's ideas

Rudyard Kipling, author and poet

Frank Lloyd Wright, architect

Jean Toomer, Black Renaissance poet

Margaret Anderson, author

Katherine Hulme, author

Katherine Mansfield, author

Minor White, photographer

Georgia O'Keeffe, painter

Zona Gale, author

Gorham Munson, editor

Moshe Feldenkreis, physicist and physiologist

Alexandro Jodorowsky, filmmaker

J.B. Priestley, author

Peter Brooks, director

and a surprising number of other public
figures who wish to remain nameless.

Further Reading

A basic overview of Gurdjieff's ideas is given in:
    Bennett, J.G., *Gurdjieff: Making a New World*. New York: Harper & Row, 1974
    Ouspensky, P.D., *In Search of the Miraculous*. New York: Harcourt, Brace and Co., 1949

Other accounts may be found in Kenneth Walker's books:
    Walker, K., *Venture with Ideas*. London: Jonathon Cape, 1951
    Walker, K., *A Study of Gurdjieff's Teaching*. London: Jonathon Cape, 1957

Gurdjieff's own works are:
    All and Everything. New York: Harcourt, Brace and Co., 1950
    Meetings with Remarkable Men. New York: E.P. Dutton and Co., 1963
    Herald of the Coming Good. Paris, 1933. Reprinted New York: Weiser, 1970
    Views from the Real World: Early Talks of Gurdjieff as Recollected by His Pupils. New York: E.P. Dutton, 1973
    Life is Real Only Then, When "I Am." New York: Privately Printed by E.P. Dutton for Triangle Editions, 1975

Accounts of personal experience with Gurdjieff are many. Particularly vivid descriptions of his personality and teaching are given in:
    de Hartmann, T., *Our Life with Mr. Gurdjieff*. New York: Cooper Square Publishers, Inc., 1964
    Peters, F., *Boyhood with Gurdjieff*. New York: E.P. Dutton and Co., 1964
    Bennett, J., *Witness*. New York: Dharma Books, 1962
    Nott, S.C., *Teachings of Gurdjieff: The Journal of a Pupil*. London: Routledge and Kegan Paul, 1964

Descriptions of Gurdjieff's teaching by his pupils, including actual teaching material, may be found in:
    Ouspensky, P.D., *The Psychology of Man's Possible Evolution*. New York, Alfred Knopf, 1954
    Ouspensky, P.D., *The Fourth Way*. New York: Alfred Knopf, 1957
    Nicoll, M., *Psychological Commentaries on the Teaching of Gurdjieff and Ouspensky*. London: Vincent Stuart, 1952

Notes

CHAPTER ONE

The quotes at the beginning of the chapter are: Saying of Mohammed; Ouspensky, P.D.: *In Search of the Miraculous,* New York, Harcourt Brace & Co., 1949.

1. Castaneda, C.: *Journey to Ixtlan.* New York; Simon and Schuster, 1973.
2. Gurdjieff, G.I.: *The Herald of the Coming Good.* Paris, 1933, (no publisher given); reprinted, New York, Weiser, 1970, p. 13.
3. Gurdjieff, G.I.: *ibid.,* p. 17.
4. Ouspensky, P.: *In Search of the Miraculous.* New York; Harcourt, Brace and Co., 1949, p. 102.
5. *Ibid.,* p. 16.
6. *Ibid.,* p. 303.
7. Idries Shah describes Gurdjieff's teachings this way in a footnote to his pamphlet, *Special Problems in the Study of Sufi Ideas,* Society for the Understanding of the Foundation of Ideas, Tunbridge Wells; 1966:

   "G.I. Gurdjieff left abundant clues to the Sufic origins of virtually every point in his 'system'; though it obviously belongs more specifically to the Khajagan (Naqshbandi) form of the dervish teaching. In addition to the practices of 'the work' such books as Gurdjieff's *Beelzebub* (otherwise known as *All and Everything,* New York 1950, 1238 pages) and *Meetings with Remarkable Men,* 2nd impression, 1963, abound with references, often semi-covert ones, to the Sufi system. He also cites by name the Naqshbandis, Kubravis and other Sufis, in his 1923 Paris 'prospectus' of a public presentation. *(The Echo of the Champs-Elysees,* 1, 37, part 2, Paris: 13–25 Dec. 1923), quoting as sources, *inter alia* the Naqshbandi, Qadiri, Kalandar, Kubravi and Mevlevi dervish practices. . . ."

8, Gurdjieff, G.I.: *Life is Real Only Then, When "I Am."* Privately printed by E.P. Dutton & Co. for Triangle Editions, New York, 1975, p. 27.
9. Actually it was the second bullet wound in Gurdjieff's accident-prone life. He reports that he had been shot in a hunting accident as a boy, an event predicted by a psychic.
10. Pauwels, L.: *Gurdjieff.* New York; Samuel Weiser, 1972, p. 31.
11. Gurdjieff, G.I.: *Life is Real Only Then, When "I Am,"* p. 20.
12. *Ibid.,* p. 23.
13. *Ibid.,* p. 24.
14. Wilson, C.: *The Outsider.* New York; Houghton Mifflin, 1967.
15. Ouspensky, P.D.: *op. cit.,* p. 7.
16. de Hartmann, T.: *Our Life with Mr. Gurdjieff.* New York: Cooper Square Publishers, 1964.
17. Gurdjieff, G.I.: *All and Everything: Beelzebub's Tales to His Grandson.* New York: Harcourt, Brace and Co., 1950.
18. Gurdjieff, G.I.: *Meetings with Remarkable Men.* New York: E.P. Dutton & Co., 1963.

19.   Gurdjieff, G.I.: *Life is Real Only Then, When "I Am," op. cit.*
20.   Gurdjieff, G.I.: *All and Everything, op. cit.*, p. v.
21.   Plewes, E.: *Guide and Index to G.I. Gurdjieff's All and Everything.* Toronto: The Society for Traditional Studies, 1971.
22.   Gurdjieff, G.I.: *Herald of the Coming Good. op. cit.*

CHAPTER TWO

The symbols at the beginning of the chapter are from:
Halevi, Z'ev ben Shimon: *An Introduction to the Cabala: Tree of Life.* New York; Samuel Weiser, Inc., 1972.
Zimmer, Heinrich: *Myths and Symbols in Indian Art and Civilization.* New York; Harper, 1962.
Graham, F. Lanier, ed.: *The Rainbow Book.* Berkeley; Shambala, 1975

1.   Ouspensky, P.D.: *In Search of the Miraculous.* New York, Harcourt Brace & Co., 1949, p. 30.
2.   *Ibid.*, p. 88.
3.   *Bhagavad Gita*, III, 27–28.
4.   After King, C.D.: *The Oragean Version.* Unpublished book, Long Valley, N.J., 1949, pp. 36–37. Readers who are particularly interested in exploring the Law of Three may find a more complete version in the section on Trialectics in the *Manual for Arica Trainers*, New York; Arica Institute, 1972. Lizelle Reymond relates the Law of Three to Samkhya philosophy in *To Live Within*, Baltimore; Penguin Books, 1973.
5.   After Reyner, J.H.: *The Diary of a Modern Alchemist.* London; Neville Spearman, 1974, p. 108. More can be found in *The Musical Scale and the Scheme of Evolution.* Oceanside, Calif., The Rosicrucian Fellowship, 1949.
6.   After King, C.D.: *op. cit.*, p. 157. A published discussion of the metabolism of the three foods appears in Ouspensky's *In Search of the Miraculous.*

CHAPTER THREE

The quotations at the beginning of the chapter are from:
Reich, W.: *Selected Writings.* New York; Farrar, 1960, p. 470.
Hume, David: *Of Abstract Ideas*, Bk. I, Part IV, Sec. IV.
Skinner, B.F.: "An Interview with Mr. Behaviorist: B.F. Skinner" in *Psychology Today* 1 (5), p. 69.

1.   Ouspensky, P.D.: *The Psychology of Man's Possible Evolution.* New York; Alfred Knopf, 1954, p. 13.
2.   Assagioli, Roberto: *Psychosynthesis: A Manual of Principles and Techniques.* New York; Viking/Compass, 1971. *An Act of Will.* New York; Viking/Compass, 1973.
3.   Skinner, B.F.: *Science and Human Behavior.* New York; MacMillan, 1953, has a good account of the point of view of stimulus-response psychology on the nature of self, which is, briefly, that it is a superfluous explanatory fiction. Gurdjieff's teachings on the self resemble Skinner's views and those of the Buddhist doctrine of *annata* and contradict the more tender minded of Western psychologists.

4.   Ouspensky, P.D.: *In Search of the Miraculous.* New York; Harcourt,
       Brace and Co., 1949, p. 21.
5.   Nicoll, M.: *Psychological Commentaries on the Teachings of Gurdjieff
       and Ouspensky.* 5 vols. London; Vincent Stuart, 1952–56, p. 52.
6.   *Ibid.*
7.   Gurdjieff, G.I.: *Herald of the Coming Good.* Paris; no publisher given,
       1933; reprinted, New York; Weiser, 1970, p. 30.
8.   Sheldon, W.: *Varieties of Human Physique: An Introduction to Constitu-
       tional Psychology.* New York; Harper, 1940 and *Varieties of Temperament:
       a Psychology of Constitutional Differences.* New York; Harper, 1942.
9.   Gurdjieff, G.I.: *Views from the Real World: Early Talks of Gurdjieff as
       Recollected by his Pupils.* New York: E.P. Dutton & Co., 1973, p. 119.
10.   *Ibid.,* p. 115.
11.   *Ibid..* p. 120.
12.   Krishnamurti, J.: *Krishnamurti's Notebook.* New York; Harper & Row,
       1976, p. 30.
13.   James, W.: *The Varieties of Religious Experience.* New York; Collier
       Books, 1961.
14.   Bucke, R.: *Cosmic Consciousness.* New York; E.P. Dutton & Co., 1901.
       Reprinted New Hyde Park, N.Y.; University Books, 1961.
15.   de Ropp, R.: *The Master Game.* New York; Delacorte Press, 1968, p. 62.
16.   Ouspensky: *op. cit.,* p. 13
17.   Castaneda, C.: *Tales of Power.* New York; Simon and Schuster, 1975.
18.   Nott, S.: *Teachings of Gurdjieff: The Journal of a Pupil.* London: Rout-
       ledge & Kegan Paul, 1961, p. 23.
19.   *Ibid.,* p. 23.
20.   Gurdjieff, G.I.: *All and Everything: Beelzebub's Tales to his Grandson.*
       New York; Harcourt, Brace & Co., 1950, p. 88.
21.   *Ibid.,* p. 1183.
22.   Shah, I.: *Tales of the Dervishes.* London: Jonathan Cape, 1967. New
       York: Dutton, 1970.
23.   Anonymous. "Finding the real self: a letter with a foreword by Karen
       Horney." *Am. J. Psychoanal.,* 1949, p. 93, as quoted in a footnote in
       Maslow, A.: *Toward a Psychology of Being.* Princeton; Van Nostrand,
       1962.
24.   Ouspensky, *op. cit.,* p. 251 ff.
25.   *Ibid.,* p. 163.

CHAPTER FOUR

The quotations at the beginning of the chapter are from:
Maslow, A.: *Toward a Psychology of Being.* 2nd ed. New York; Van Nostrand,
1968, p. 173.
Shah, I.: *The Way of the Sufi.* New York; Dutton, 1969, p. 155.

1.   Ouspensky, P.D.: *In Search of the Miraculous.* New York: Harcourt
       Brace & Co., 1949, p. 363.
2.   *Ibid.,* p. 200.
3.   de Ropp, R.: *Conversations with Mme. Ouspensky: 1939–40 at Lyme.*
       Far West Press, 1974.

4. Long-chen-pa: *Kindly Bent to Ease Us*. Trans. by H. Guenther. Emery-
    ville, Calif.; Dharma Press, 1975.

5. Nott, S.: *Journey Through This World: Meetings with Gurdjieff, Orage
    and Ouspensky*. London: Routledge & Kegan Paul, 1969.

6. Satprem: *Sri Aurobindo or the Adventure in Consciousness*. Pondicherry;
    Sri Aurobindo Ashram, 1970, p. 91.

7. Lutyens, M.: *Krishnamurti: The Years of Awakening*. New York; Farrar
    Strauss, 1975, p. 158.

8. Muktananda, S.: *Chitshakti Vilas: The Play of Consciousness*. Ganesh-
    puri: Sri Gurudev Ashram, 1972, p. 162.

9. Luk, C.: *The Transmission of Mind Outside the Teaching*. New York:
    Grove Press, 1974, p. 19.

10. Gurdjieff, G.I.: *All and Everything: Beelzebub's Tales to his Grandson*.
    New York: Harcourt, Brace & Co., 1950.

11. Ouspensky, P.D.: *op. cit.*, p. 250.

CHAPTER FIVE

The quotations at the beginning of the chapter are from:
Shafii, M.: "The pir (Sufi guide) and the Western psychotherapist." *R.M.
Bucke Memorial Society Newsletter Review*, 3; 9–19.
Kafka, F.: *The Great Wall of China: Stories and Reflections*. New York:
Schoeken Books, 1970, p. 162.

1. Gurdjieff, G.I.: *Views from the Real World: Early Talks of Gurdjieff as
    Recollected by his Pupils*. New York; E.P. Dutton & Co., 1973, p. 70.

2. Ouspensky, P.D.: *In Search of the Miraculous*. New York; Harcourt,
    Brace & Co., 1949, p. 37.

3. *Ibid.*, p. 39.

4. Martin, D.M.: "Account of the Sarmoun Brotherhood," in Davidson,
    R.W., ed.: *Documents of Contemporary Dervish Communities*. Society
    for Organizing Unified Research in Cultural Education; London, 1966,
    p. 23.

5. Ouspensky, P.D.: *The Psychology of Man's Possible Evolution*. New
    York; Alfred Knopf, 1954, p. 280.

6. King, C.D.: *The Oragean Version*. Unpublished book. Long Valley, N.J.;
    1949, p. 94.

7. Shah, I.: "The Story of Mushkil Gusha," in *Caravan of Dreams*. London;
    Octagon Press, 1968, p. 117.

8. de Ropp, R.: *Church of the Earth*. New York; Delta Books, 1974, p. 55.

9. Nicoll, M.: *Psychological Commentaries on the Teachings of Gurdjieff
    and Ouspensky*. 5 vols. London; Vincent Stuart, 1952–56, p. 457.

10. Tracol, H.: *George Ivanovitch Gurdjieff: Man's Awakening and the
    Practice of Remembering Oneself*. Bray; Guild Press, 1968.

11. Gurdjieff, G.I.: *op. cit.*, p. 240.

12. de Ropp, R.: *Conversations with Mme. Ouspensky: 1939–40 at Lyme*.
    Far West Press, 1974.

13. Nicoll, M.: *op. cit.*, p. 456.

14. Gurdjieff, G.I.: *op. cit.*, p. 98.

15. *Ibid.*, p. 92.

16. de Hartmann, T.: *Our Life with Mr. Gurdjieff.* New York; Cooper Square Publishers, 1964, p. 42.

17. Ouspensky, P.D.: *op. cit.*, p. 268. More information on chief feature may be found in the enneagrams of fixations, passions, virtues and ideas given in Lilly, J. and Hart, J.: "The Arica Training," in Tart, C., ed.: *Transpersonal Psychologies.* New York: Harper & Row, 1974, pp. 331-351. The bare bones of a very powerful system for working on chief feature are given in this article. The full system is taught orally at Arica and SAT.

18. Nott, C.S.: *Teachings of Gurdjieff: The Journal of a Pupil.* London: Routledge & Kegan Paul, 1961.

19. Nicoll: *op. cit.*, p. 695.

20. Gurdjieff, G.I.: *op. cit.*, p. 92.

21. Nicoll: *op. cit.*, p. 696.

22. Gurdjieff, G.I.: *op. cit.*, p. 100.

23. Peters, F.: *Boyhood with Gurdjieff.* New York; E.P. Dutton & Co., 1964, p. 72.

24. Gurdjieff, G.I.: *op. cit.*, p. 95.

25. After Ouspensky, P.D.: 1949, *op. cit.*, p. 282.

26. Ouspensky, P.D.: 1949, *op. cit.*, p. 354.

27. Gurdjieff, G.I.: *op. cit.*, p. 160.

28. Martin, D.: "Account of the Sarmoun Brotherhood," in Davidson, R., ed.: *Documents on Contemporary Dervish Communities.* London; Society for Organizing Unified Research as Cultural Education, 1966, p. 22.

29. Ouspensky: 1949, *op. cit.*, p. 235.

30. *Ibid.*, p. 49.

31. Ouspensky, P.D.: 1954: *op. cit.*, p. 19.

32. Orage, A.R.: *The Active Mind.* New York; Heritage House, 1954, p. 12.

33. *Ibid.*, p. 94.

CHAPTER SIX

The quotations at the beginning of the chapter are from:
Freud, S.: "The future prospects of psychoanalytic therapy," in Reif, P., ed.: *Therapy and Technique.* New York; Collier Books, 1963, p. 82.
Priestley, J.B.: *Man and Time,* New York; Doubleday & Co., 1964, p. 264.
Rumi in Shah, I.: *The Way of the Sufi.* New York; Dutton & Co., 1970, p. 31.

1. Tracol, H.: *George Ivanovitch Gurdjieff: Man's Awakening and the Practice of Remembering Oneself.* Bray; Guild Press, 1968, p. 5.

2. Bennett, J.B.: *Prospectus of the International Academy for Continuous Education.* Sherborne; The Institute for the Comparative Study of History, Philosophy and the Sciences Limited, 1972.

3. *Prospectus of the Claymont Society for Continuous Education.* The Claymont Society for Continuous Education, Inc. (no date).

4. Nott, C.S.: *Journey Through this World: Meetings with Gurdjieff, Orage and Ouspensky.* London: Routledge & Kegan Paul, 1969.

5. Twombly, R.C.: "Organic Living: Frank Lloyd Wright's Taliesin Fellow-

ship and Georgi Gurdjieff's Institute for the Harmonious Development
of Man," *Wisconsin Magazine of History*, Winter 1974–75, pp. 126–139.

6.   Nott: *op. cit.*
7.   Peters, F.: quoted in Twombly, *op. cit.*, p. 137.
8.   de Ropp, R.: *Church of the Earth.* New York; Delta Books, 1974, p. 43
9.   *New York Times:* Aug. 5, 1975, p. 22.
10. de Ropp: *op. cit.*, pp. 156–157.